PLANT CLOSINGS

International Context and Social Costs

**Carolyn C. Perrucci • Robert Perrucci
Dena B. Targ • Harry R. Targ**

ALDINE DE GRUYTER
New York

ABOUT THE AUTHORS

Carolyn C. Perrucci is Professor of Sociology, Department of Sociology and Anthropology, and Chair of the interdisciplinary program in Women's Studies, Purdue University.

Robert Perrucci is Professor of Sociology, Department of Sociology and Anthropology, Purdue University.

Dena B. Targ is Associate Professor and Extension Specialist, Department of Child Development and Family Studies, Purdue University

Harry R. Targ is a Professor in the Department of Political Science and member of the Committee on American Studies, Purdue University.

ALDINE DE GRUYTER
A Division of Walter de Gruyter, Inc.
200 Saw Mill River Road
Hawthorne, New York 10532

Library of Congress Cataloging-in-Publication Data
Plant closings : international context and social costs / Carolyn C.
    Perrucci . . . [et al.].
    p. cm. —(Social institutions and social change)
    Bibliography: p.
    Includes index.
    ISBN 0-202-30338-1 (lib. bdg.) ISBN 0-202-30339-X (pbk.)
    1. Plant shutdowns—United States.   2. Plant shutdowns.
3. Unemployment—United States—Psychological aspects.
4. Unemployment—Psychological aspects.   5. Work and family—United
States.   6. Work and family.   I. Perrucci, Carolyn Cummings.
II. Series.
HD5708.55.U6P5195   1988   88-391
338.6'042—dc19   CIP

Printed in the United States of America
10 9 8 7 6 5 4 3 2 1

Cover by Sonja Originals
Photograph by Edward F. Johnston

CONTENTS

PREFACE

This book is a product of our interest as scholars in the political economy of work and family and of our concern as activists for advancing the rights of working women and men to a secure job, a decent income, and a greater measure of control over the social organization of their work. Our research on plant closings was carried out within the context of a broader set of socioeconomic changes that are transforming the world economy.

We have located this study within the international and national political economy that impacts upon the lives of workers in every factory and office across the country. We have made this connection to demonstrate to scholars, activists, and workers the causes of, and needed remedies for, the human and social costs of plant closings.

A great many people helped us in carrying out our studies. We could not have embarked on our plant closing project without the assistance of organized labor. Don Scheiber, AFL-CIO community services representative to United Way, served as our "sponsor" to the union leadership involved in plant closings in Indiana. Through his contacts we obtained the cooperation of Martin Mummert, President of Local #3154 of the United Brotherhood of Carpenters and Joiners, and Don Strock, International Vice-President of the Retail, Wholesale and Department Store Union (RWSDU) and Jerry Graves, Vice President of RWSDU Local #1976. The members of the Workers Aid Council of Local #3154, particularly Harold Brigance, Wilma Brigance, and Barbara McCoy, shared their time and information with us. Personal support and encouragement for our research by Lawrence Mayberry of the State AFL-CIO office in Indianapolis provided the basis for some financial assistance for our work.

We wish to thank the Indiana State AFL-CIO, Robert L. Ringel, Purdue University Vice-President and Dean of the Graduate School, and Robert Whitford, Director of Purdue's Center for Public Policy and Public Administration for financial support for this research. We also thank C. P. Daniels and the late Dewey Cummings Daniels for financial contributions to the Labor Studies Research Group which was founded by the authors. Dena Targ also acknowledges the support of research time

ix

by the Agricultural Experiment Station, Purdue University. Special thanks are extended to graduate students for assistance throughout the many phases of this project. They are: Peter Cunningham, Fur-Jen Denq, Stephen Duncan, Robert Garza, Joseph Ignagni, Cliff Speckman, Kerry Stephenson, Sarah Weiser, and Dorothy Wheeler. Lori Miller, the research assistant who ably handled all aspects of data preparation and analysis deserves a separate thanks. Mary Perigo worked with us throughout the project handling many tasks including production of questionnaires, interview schedules, and manuscript preparation. She did an outstanding job of transcribing lengthy tapes of interviews and group meetings that help to add a human dimension to our statistics. We also acknowledge the help of Denise Howard, Marcy Rhodes, and Kay Solomon in the preparation of the final manuscript.

We wish to note that the authors are collaborators on a series of studies on labor. The order of authorship for this book is alphabetical and does not reflect any distinction in responsibility or contribution.

Finally, we thank our children Alissa Cummings Perrucci, Martin Cummings Perrucci, and Rebecca Michelle Targ for their tolerance and good humor in living with parents who blend work, friendship, and politics so as to require many working "dinners" and project "vacations." We hope that we have set a good example for them.

Carolyn C. Perrucci
Robert Perrucci
Dena B. Targ
Harry R. Targ

INTRODUCTION: THE SIGNIFICANCE OF PLANT CLOSINGS

As this introduction was being written several business events were receiving national coverage. One of the nation's major steel companies, LTV Corporation, filed for bankruptcy. Faced with less demand from domestic markets and increased competition from foreign producers, steel companies in the United States were described as being in deep trouble. General Motors, the giant of the auto industry, announced plans for the closing of eleven plants, thereby displacing 29,000 workers. This move was apparently undertaken to offset problems of growing inventories and declining market share.

At about the same time that LTV was going under and GM was closing plants, the nation's No. 1 steelmaker, U.S. Steel, was changing its name to USX Corporation. The name change was more than symbolic, as it reflected USX's diversification into oil and gas production, which now accounts for about one-half of its business. Some of the billions of dollars spent by USX to acquire oil and gas companies came from wage and benefit concessions, which were extracted from workers.

These three front-page business news stories are but small indications of a more fundamental change that is reshaping the U.S. economy and work force. The manufacturing base of the economy, namely, steel, automobiles, electronics, textiles, and rubber has been steadily declining. Rather than investing money in replacement plants and new production technology, major corporations have been closing older plants and investing in other areas of the economy, and opening new plants in lower wage labor markets within and outside the United States.

1

As manufacturing has declined, the so-called high-tech and service sectors have grown. Employment in these areas is generally non-union and wage rates are far below those found in unionized manufacturing jobs. Workers who are displaced from plant closings or unemployed due to scaled-down manufacturing plants, as well as new entrants into the labor market, are faced with fewer employment opportunities generally or with sharp reductions in income if they find a job.

All indications are that these changes in the economy are not temporary, and are likely to accelerate in the next decade. It seems likely that the next decade will see a continuation of the integration of the United States into the world economy, and not necessarily as the dominant economic actor. This is expected to result in continued job loss in manufacturing through labor-replacing technology, investment in foreign operations, and the movement of U.S. production facilities to Third World countries.

The evidence for these changes is not buried in obscure academic reports, but appears frequently on the pages of newspapers and mass media magazines. The June 23, 1986 issue of *Time* magazine features a story entitled "Singing the Shutdown Blues," in which were reported the following facts:

- In 1983 there were one million steelworkers. Today there are 650,000, with projected declines of another 15% by 1995.
- The U.S. Department of Labor has projected the addition of 16 million new jobs between 1984 and 1995. Almost 90% of these jobs will be in the service sector.
- There has been a "hollowing out" of many U.S. manufacturing companies in that they have become reassembly plants for foreign products. Even in domestic auto plants, 15% of the parts used (e.g., engines and transmissions) are produced outside the United States.
- Since 1979, 100 textile and apparel plants were closed in North Carolina with the resultant loss of 25,000 jobs.

Despite this listing, the *Time* article has an "up-beat" tone. For example, the subtitle of the article is: *"U.S. industry undergoes a wrenching change, but it could be for the good,"* which suggests that these changes may be part of a healthy, growing economy (". . . the very dynamism of the American industrial transition . . ."). Such a view is similar to that of the late Harvard economist Joseph Schumpeter who saw economic dislocations such as plant closings as exemplary of "creative destruction," eliminating inefficient operations and providing new economic opportunities.

Public discussion about plant closings by policy makers, business representatives, scholars, and labor leaders has focused upon a series of important questions, such as, why plants close and what the consequences of such closings are for workers, their families, and communities. We have used these questions as a guide for this study. Our purpose is to improve understanding of the social and economic changes that impact upon workers today and the way in which they, in turn, are responding to such changes.

On December 1, 1982, an RCA television cabinet-making factory in Monticello, Indiana, closed its doors for the last time. Four hundred and fifty workers immediately lost their jobs, adding to 400 workers that had already been laid off. The town had a population of 5000, within White County, with a population of 23,000. RCA was the second largest employer in the county. About 55% of the work force was female, the average age of those displaced was 44 years, and the median number of years worked at RCA was 14.

This book focuses on this plant closing in order to learn something about how it happened and what its consequences were both for displaced workers and others living in Monticello. However, we have designed this case study around a series of questions that have far-reaching implications for American society and the casualties of a changing economic order. A brief discussion of the questions around which this book is structured follows.

Why Do Plants Close?

As noted above, conventional wisdom views today's plant closings as part of a continuing pattern of normal change in the U.S. economy. While there may be a decline in the larger, unionized manufacturing industries there is growth of smaller, more productive firms that are better able to compete in the world economy. It is believed that the economy that emerges from these changes will be reinvigorated, more innovative, and better adapted to today's circumstances. For example, McKenzie (1984, p. 85) states: "As some firms go under, they release their resources to other, more cost-effective firms that offer consumers more of what they want at more attractive prices."

Some analysts have traced the decline in heavy industry, especially in steel, to a failure to use the latest technological innovations that would make American products more competitive with steel produced abroad.

Plants in Japan and West Germany are newer and more modern, and thus able to have a competitive advantage in international markets.

Another variant of the "technological inadequacy" perspective points out that as a nation we have failed to invest enough of our resources in research and development activities that help to maintain a high level of innovation across many different industrial areas. While American R & D expenditures (both in the private and public sectors) appear to be proportionately equal to or greater than those of our main European and Far Eastern competitors, more money is disproportionately allocated to research and development in the military sector, thus limiting the contribution to innovations in the civilian sector (Dumas, 1986).

A major challenge to the above-stated ideas is found in the views of Bluestone and Harrison (1982) who have pointed instead to the hypermobility of capital in pursuit of higher profit margins. Declining rates of profit across all sectors of the U.S. economy have "pushed" capital in search of better returns. The "pull" has been investment opportunities and cheaper labor in Third World countries. The result of these "push-pull" factors has been capital flight and disinvestment in major U.S. industries.

While we cannot answer definitively the question of why the RCA plant in Monticello closed when it did, we can locate that closing within the context of international, national, and local economic conditions. Chapters 2 and 3 discuss these economic conditions and further our understanding of the reasons responsible for the general pattern of plant closings across the United States.

Is There a "New" Unemployment?

There has been some tendency, especially by political figures, to downplay the significance of the persistently high levels of unemployment in the U.S. during the past decade (Targ, 1983). Although there are 7 million officially unemployed workers today, the problems they face are not felt to be as great as those experienced by unemployed workers earlier in this century, especially during the 1930s. The alleged reason for the difference is that unemployed workers today have a "safety net" that buffers the economic or psychological impact of joblessness. Unemployment insurance, private- and employer-initiated health plans, community social services, and private sector assistance programs for persons in need are more available today in contrast to earlier historical periods.

A second reason for suggesting that today's unemployed are "new" or "different" is that women now constitute almost one-half of the labor force and thus are well represented among the unemployed. It is often felt that because many women in the labor force are second earners, their families are less dependent on their income. When these second earners lose their jobs the family may be denied discretionary income for family "extras" like vacations, but they do not face the hardship of not being able to pay for necessities.

In addition, female workers are often viewed as having weaker identification than men with their work as an important or central life interest. Thus, job loss for many women should not result in negative psychological consequences stemming from loss of meaningful work, self-esteem, or valued social relationships.

However, there is another sense in which today's unemployment is "new" or different from that of earlier times. Unemployment due to a downturn in the business cycle has long been accepted as a normal feature of a market economy. Declining demand for goods and services results in reduced production and temporary layoff of workers. Those who become unemployed because of cyclical downturns are not considered to be displaced, because they will probably be recalled to work when economic conditions improve.

Structural unemployment, in contrast to cyclical unemployment, occurs when workers are told that their jobs are gone. This kind of unemployment can occur when machiners are being used to do work that was formerly carried out by human labor, or because of plant closings or relocation. One of the most severe problems of unemployment today is that workers displaced from manufacturing industries do not have new jobs to which they can look forward. They experience prolonged unemployment, and if they become reemployed it is because they are forced into jobs at lower pay, status, and security (Office of Technology Assessment, 1986).

In Chapters 4 and 5 we compare displaced male and female workers in terms of economic, social, and psychological impacts of joblessness. We examine the extent to which men and women differ in their experience of unemployment and in their reentry into the ranks of the employed.

How Are Communities Affected by Plant Closings?

Recently, studies of the effects of unemployment have limited their attention to the unemployed workers themselves and, less frequently, to workers' families. This has probably been because such studies were often based on samples of unemployed persons from across the nation or from many large metropolitan areas (see, e.g., Schlozman and Verba, 1979). Thus, the study of the experience of being unemployed was removed from the actual context in which the unemployment took place and in which the unemployed person would have to seek reemployment.

However, some attention to plant closings in small- and medium-sized cities has made it possible to trace the effects of closings far beyond displaced workers. According to the report by the Office of Technology Assessment (1986, p. 10), for example, "Displacement can be devastating for communities and regions as well as individuals. . . . Large losses of employment have ripple effects in the community. A large layoff in one industry also affects workers in supplier industries and workers in local service establishments when laidoff workers reduce spending."

Depending upon the size of the community relative to the size of a plant that has closed, a community will suffer a loss in payroll taxes, property taxes, and charitable donations to community projects. Moreover, this loss of revenue will occur at a time when there is both increased need for public assistance for the unemployed and increased demand for public expenditures to keep existing industries within the community and at the same time attract new industry. Thus, in describing some of the policy alternatives for communities faced with a plant closing, McKenzie (1984) contends that they must actively promote the community to a prospective new industry with a combination of positive thinking and economic incentives.

> Every time a city complains bitterly about its economic distress, it can be assured that some company decides to locate elsewhere; it can be certain that other communities elsewhere are pleased because industrial recruitment has for them been made just a little easier. Another perhaps less obvious solution is for the community to remain competitive in terms of taxes and services delivered. We have stressed that profit-maximizing firms will not allow their capital to go down the economic drain. Keeping taxes in line with the taxes paid by other companies in other communities ensures firms of an equal chance of competing in their markets (McKenzie, 1984, p. 183).

Thus, we have the prospect of communities being caught between competing needs for services by the unemployed and demands of the business community to attract new industry. The likely result of a shutdown is an erosion of social services for the needy and an increased tax burden on remaining industries and individuals.

At about the same time that a community's political and economic leaders are trying to hold existing industries and attract new ones, even the employed workers are likely to become anxious about their own job security. Research findings reported by Brenner (1973), Marshall and Funch (1979), Catalano and Dooley (1977, 1979), and Dooley *et al.* (1981) all suggest a relationship between unemployment rates for some aggregate unit (e.g., county, metropolitan area) and the psychological well-being of the general population (e.g., admission to state mental hospitals, or reported depression in samples of nonhospitalized persons).

In Chapter 3 we examine the hypothesis that plant closings will be followed by "ripple effects," which bring economic and social stress to segments of the community beyond displaced workers themselves.

How Are Displaced Workers Affected?

The focus of most research on the effects of individual unemployment or mass unemployment due to a plant closing is upon economic, social, and psychological consequences. Although there is general agreement that the immediate effect of unemployment is income loss, there is disagreement about the severity of that loss and its consequences. Some displaced workers may have either sufficient savings or become reemployed soon enough to limit the amount and significance of income loss. Other workers may lack any savings and may therefore experience severe economic crisis with the loss of even one month's income.

McKenzie (1984) takes the uncommon position that despite immediate hardship, displaced workers may enjoy some special opportunities and benefits. He states:

> Many people lose their jobs when plants are closed, but their loss does not necessarily mean that they are somehow worse off. Workers unemployed because their plants close are also beneficiaries of the competitive process (involving closings and openings) in other markets, which yields higher quality goods at lower prices. Workers unemployed because of their firms' failures can sometimes find other jobs in expanding sectors of the economy—in those firms that are winning the competitive struggle. Furthermore, workers unemployed by plant closings are often compensated in advance for their expected loss in income when their plants close. When the risk of plant closing is high, the supply of labor is often restricted (who would prefer to work where the loss of employ-

ment is highly probable or imminent?). As a result, in those risky jobs wages are comparatively high, with the wage differential providing a form of prepaid compensation for the risk of unemployment (McKenzie, 1984, p. 87).

There is also disagreement about how unemployment affects the families of displaced workers, but that may be because there has been relatively little research about the subject. One study in a midwestern city of a population of 70,000 by Larson (1984) compared couples in which the husbands were employed with couples having unemployed husbands. Unemployed couples reported lower marital adjustment and poorer marital communication. On the other hand, a similar comparison by Buss and Redburn (1983) revealed little relationship between husbands' unemployment status and wives' and childrens' mental health. Finally, Perrucci and Targ (1987) obtained information from 75 displaced blue-collar workers at 1, 5, and 9 months after their factory closed. Workers' marital status remained stable over the 8-month period, and marital happiness, family cohesion, and family adaptability declined only slightly.

The psychological effects of unemployment have been studied extensively and, once again, with mixed results. Several studies (Kasl and Cobb, 1979; Buss and Redburn, 1983) report only modest levels of stress (e.g., depression, loss of self-esteem) among displaced workers following a plant closing. They also report that there is adaptation to the loss of work role soon after the initial period of unemployment. A review of these research findings by Perrucci and Perrucci (1986) suggests that the severity and duration of displaced workers' psychological distress following unemployment may be related to the regional or national economic climate. When workers perceive economic conditions as favorable they are optimistic about reemployment opportunities and thereby feel less threatened by their job loss.

Chapters 4 and 5 examine the economic, social, and psychological effects of the plant closing on displaced workers and their families. Our analyses contribute to a greater understanding of the complex nature of postemployment stress.

What Is the Political Response of Displaced Workers?

As we have noted, job loss results in a wide range of far-reaching change in the lives of displaced workers. In addition to possible economic loss, family disruption, and altered self-concepts, unemployed women and men inevitably think about themselves in relation to the larger society. How does their experience affect their own values and beliefs about the virtue of hard work or the American Dream of equality of opportunity? Is their confidence in local and national social institutions shaken? Are they attracted to "radical" solutions to the problems of the unemployed? Or, do they withdraw from social life to seek inward-looking solutions or other-worldly goals?

We expect that workers who are laid-off or fired as part of a partial cut-back might accept their situation with resignation or perhaps even self-blame. Since almost everyone else at the plant is still working it is difficult to level blame at the plant owners or managers, or at the larger economic system. However, when a total plant closes workers are likely to look beyond themselves for an answer to "why." There may be both individual and collective examination of unions, corporate power, or the failure of elected officials to deal with the needs of workers.

Chapter 6 examines the patterns of social relationships, social values, and political attitudes of displaced workers. We discuss these patterns as an indicator of "social integration"—those relationships and beliefs that may reflect the strength or weakness of ties to existing social institutions. Of special concern is whether there are variations in social integration for workers of different age, gender, prior experience with unemployment, and current employment status.

Chapter 7 examines a specific type of political response of displaced workers, namely, worker consciousness. Because of the way in which plant closings occur, the spatial concentration of workers, and the mobilization of discontent during closing negotiations, plant closings present a special opportunity to examine the structural and social psychological factors that aid or inhibit the development of worker consciousness.

What Can Be Done About Plant Closings and the Needs of Displaced Workers?

The final chapter of this book reviews the main findings of our research and examines a range of policy alternatives to deal with the problems of plant closings and the range of political responses workers have engaged in to forestall or overcome closings. One set of policies is concerned with either limiting the ease with which capital mobility occurs or providing compensation to communities and workers as a cost of closing. The second set of policies is aimed at assisting workers and their families through the period of unemployment and preparing them for new employment opportunities. Taken together, these remedies are aimed at developing a new industrial policy that facilitates the allocation of human and material resources in a humane and rational fashion.

A Note on Method

The research on which this book is based was carried out in 1983 and 1984. After the RCA plant in Monticello closed in December of 1982, the four co-authors decided to conduct an in-depth study of the causes and consequences of the closing. We used a variety of methodologies and data sources in order to develop as complete an understanding as possible, given the limitations of time and funds. The study was carried out in three stages.

Stage One

Soon after the RCA plant closing, the research team contacted the President of Local 3154 of the United Brotherhood of Carpenters and Joiners (UBCJ). Contact was made through a union representative to the Northwest Central Labor Council who accompanied the research team to meet the President at the union hall in Monticello.

For a period of about 3 months, on a weekly basis, one or more members of the research team visited the UBCJ union hall for purposes of observation, informal discussion, and formal interviews with members of the union's Workers Aid Council (WAC), a group designed to assist workers with a wide variety of economic and personal problems connected with the closing. Information obtained during this period was very valuable in terms of understanding workers' perceptions of the reasons for the closing, the role played by community leaders before, during, and after the closing, and the way that workers and their families were being affected.

During this period we also obtained copies of all news stories, editorials, etc., that appeared in the local newspaper concerning the plant closing. These news accounts start with the initial announcement in June 1982 that RCA was considering closing the plant and continue through the early months of 1983, after the closing. These materials served as one source for documenting the chronology of events surrounding the closing and for obtaining the names of persons from labor, business, and political groups involved in discussions about the closing.

Stage Two

The second stage of the project covers a period from March through July of 1983. During this time we continued our visits to the union hall and we worked with the Workers' Aid Council in the planning and preparation of a meeting between WAC and a variety of public officials. WAC invited Indiana's two U.S. Senators, the U.S. Representative from the district, the area Representative to the State Legislature, the Mayor of Monticello, and the chairperson of the community's Economic Development Committee to a meeting to discuss the actions that were being undertaken at the local, state, and national level to deal with the problems of communities like Monticello and the plight of displaced workers.

During this period formal interviews were conducted with 38 owners/managers of local businesses (those located "on the square" in downtown Monticello) and 15 prominent community members. The latter group included the mayor, members of the city council, union leaders, members of the Chamber of Commerce, directors of social service agencies, clergy, members of the Economic Development Committee, and the publisher of a local newspaper. These interviews focused on the following: (a) why the plant closed, (b) efforts made to keep the plant from closing, (c) actual and expected impact of the closing on Monticello, and (d) what other communities might learn from the Monticello experience.

During this time we also started to collect archival data for a period preceding and following the closing for the county in which Monticello is located and for a "matching" county. These data include aggregate health/morbidity statistics, juvenile court records, crisis center logs, welfare statistics, and family court records.

Stage Three

The final phase of data collection occurred during August and September of 1983. A mail questionnaire was distributed to 686 RCA workers (including those who were working and those already on layoff) who were displaced at the time of the closing and were covered under the closing agreement. The list of workers covered by the contract was obtained from the president of the Local 3154 of UBCJ. It is likely that some unknown number of workers left town after the closing and that many of those to whom questionnaires were sent did not receive them. A total of 327 usable questionnaires was received, for a 48% return rate.

A very similar questionnaire was distributed to 95 employed workers in another manufacturing plant in Monticello (42 or 44% usable questionnaires were returned). The plant was selected because of the similar skill level of its employees with those of the RCA workers. These workers were used as a "control group" for the purpose of comparing unemployed RCA workers with employed workers on a number of factors. Since we did not have "before" and "after" measures for the RCA workers, comparison with controls and retrospective questions for RCA workers were used to attribute to the plant closing experience selected effects on workers.

During the period in which data were being gathered and analyzed we maintained contact with different labor groups in order to provide them with information that they might find useful. Our research team also worked with the Monticello local and the Northwest Central Labor Council in preparing a proposal for state funding of a job club. The proposal was funded and the Monticello union played a central role with professional staff in setting up training sessions about seeking new employment. The job club was established in the local union hall in Monticello and was successful in assisting a significant number of displaced workers in learning job searching skills. The research team also assisted the Northwest Central Indiana Labor Council, AFL-CIO, with the preparation of plant closing legislation to be introduced into the state legislature.

2

PLANT CLOSINGS AND ECONOMIC CHANGE: GLOBAL, NATIONAL, AND REGIONAL CONTEXTS

The Foundations of American Capitalism on a Worldwide Basis Since World War II

The American assumption of a dominant position in the global political economy after World War II resulted from the incredible destructiveness of the war over vast stretches of Europe and Asia and the economic growth experienced by the United States as a result of the enormous demand for war material. The destructiveness was manifested in numerous ways. In Eastern Europe food production was halted, industrial production dropped below prewar levels, and class struggles intensified as traditional aristocratic rulers could no longer reestablish political control of their homelands. The Soviet Union suffered massive destruction, the most devastating of the war, but Western Europe was in shambles as well (Targ, 1986).

The economic condition of the United States was diametrically opposed to that of Europe. One estimate of comparative U.S. strength just after the war suggested that the United States had three quarters of the *world's* invested capital and two-thirds of its industrial capacity. The United States provided a large share of the industrial production to carry out the war effort and bore a smaller comparative cost in human lives and devastation of land and industrial capacity. In fact, war mobilization brought the American economy out of the most serious depression in its history. Between 1938 and 1943, at the height of wartime production, total manufacturing production increased by 2½ times. During the early postwar years, manufacturing production was roughly double what it had been before World War II. Similarly, American exports increased from totals of about $3 billion in the 1930s to $10 billion in 1945 and $14 billion in 1947 (Paterson, 1973, p. 6).

Measured by most indicators, American economic dominance in the world economy was complete. The magnitude of the American economy can be partially illustrated by the fact that in 1950, 2 years after the onset of the Marshall Plan and 5 years after the end of the war, the American gross national product was three times greater than that of the Soviet Union, and at least six times greater than all of the U.S. allies (Organski, 1965, pp. 210–212).

The transformation of the world economy was paralleled by a transformation of the American economy itself. Dramatic new levels of concentration and centralization occurred during and after World War II. Wartime governmental policies stimulated the growth of America's largest corporations by awarding contracts to them—$175 billion was awarded to some 18,539 corporations between June, 1940 and September, 1944. Two-thirds of this money ($117 billion) went to the top 100 corporations; 30% to the top 10 corporations, 12% to the next 10 and in total, 30 corporations received 49% of the total of the prime defense contracts. The top recipient was General Motors which alone received $13.8 billion or 8% of the total of defense contract work (Pursell, 1972).

The defense contracting system of World War II exacerbated a process of concentration that was already well developed. For example, the 100 leading corporations in 1935 had already produced one-third of the total product of goods in the U.S. in that year. The largest American corporations were the major benefactors of subcontracts, tax-supported plant construction, and research and development funds. The effect of wartime government policy led to an increase in working capital for the 802 corporations listed on the Securities and Exchange Commission from $8.6 billion in 1939 to $14.1 billion in June, 1945—an increase of 64%. A government report, which gathered this data, summarized the implications of their findings;

> . . . economic concentration will probably be higher in the postwar years than before the war as a result of: the production improvements and scientific research which big business gained during the war; the increase in the liquid funds and general financial strength of big business to keep its name and trademarks before the public eye during the war; and finally, the fact that big business will probably acquire a greater share of the war-built facilities which it operated than will small business, regardless of whether economic conditions are prosperous or depressed (Pursell, 1972, p. 177).

Therefore, the global experience of war set the stage for a buoyant American economy to define the character of the postwar international economic and political order. The United States had the technology, the industrial plant, the scientific expertise, and the work force to produce for the world. Further the largest corporations in America had been the major beneficiaries of the war effort. To ensure the enhancement of this worldwide distribution of resources, the United States used its political leverage and foreign policy to build a world order maximizing opportunities for American capital.

The results of American economic growth, technological change, the emergence of multinational corporations, and U.S. foreign policy were enormous expansion in foreign trade and investment. The dollar value of American exports rose from $10.3 billion in 1950 to $143.7 billion in 1978 and foreign investments rose from $11.8 billion to $168.0 billion (Blake and Walters, 1976, p. 78; U.S. Department of Commerce, Bureau of the Census, 1951, 1979, 1980, 1981). U.S. banking assets overseas grew from $3.5 billion in 1960 to $155 billion in 1974 (Hawley, 1978). Despite the mounting crisis in the American and world economy by the 1970s, the United States still accounted for about 60% of the world's foreign private investment in 1970. Twenty-three of the 50 largest multinational corporations in 1975 were American owned; four of the top ten corporations were American oil companies (Modelski, 1978, pp. 46–47).

The United States and Global Political Economy in Crisis

The American economic success story was based on the enormous productivity increases of World War II and dramatically escalated foreign investment and trade after the war. However, by the 1970s it became clear that the dominant position of the United States in the world economy was changing.

A comparison of the United States position in 1950 with other world actors indicated that America's Gross National Product (GNP) was three times larger than that of the Soviet Union, six times larger than that of Great Britain, nine times larger than that of France and Germany, and twelve times larger than that of Japan. In 1978, the American Gross National Product was only 1.7 times larger than that of the Soviet Union, 7.8 times larger than that of Great Britain, 5 times larger than that of France, 3.6 times larger than that of West Germany, and 2.7 times larger than that of Japan (U.S. Department of Commerce, Bureau of the Census, 1981). Essentially the relative position of the United States as compared to each of these countries declined, with the exception of Great Britain.

Other indicators tell the same story. In 1950, six western countries (Canada, France, West Germany, Italy, Japan, and Great Britain) had a combined Gross Domestic Product equal to three-fourths that of the United States. By 1979, the combined Gross Domestic Product of these countries exceeded the United States by 20%. Considering the six countries, the growth rates in Gross National Product between 1970 and 1978 of Canada (143%), France (135%), and Japan (152%) exceeded that of the United States (129%). In fact, growth in Gross National Product of Bulgaria (134%), China (170%), Poland (153%), Romania (171%), and the Soviet Union (137%) also outpaced that of the United States (U.S. Department of Commerce, Bureau of the Census, 1981, p. 878).

Looking at indicators of relative productivity and trade in Table 2.1, confirms further the declining economic advantage of the United States. America's share of world production of oil and iron declined precipitously, as did basic steel production. Even the share of world production of coal declined. As an indicator of manufacturing dominance, the production of automobiles declined from a near world monopoly in 1950 to less than one-third of the world's share in the 1970s. Finally, the declining U.S. share of world production of raw materials and

Table 2.1. Indicators of Relative United States Economic Capabilities: 1950–1978 (U.S. Total as Percentage of World Total)

Indicator	1950	1960	1970	1975	1978
Crude petroleum production	51	33	21	16	14
Crude steel production	46	26	20	16	18
Iron ore production	43	19	13	9	10
Coal production	35	20	26	24	22
Wheat production	17	15	12	16	11
Passenger cars	82	52	29	27	29
International financial reserves	49	21	16	07[a]	—
Exports	17	16	14	12	11

[a] 1976 data.

Source: U.N., Statistical Yearbook, several years; and Krasner, 1982, p. 38.

manufactured goods was matched by a decline in U.S. dominance in international trade and financial reserve position. Consequently, while U.S. aggregate productivity had grown since World War II, the flexibility of being the overwhelmingly dominant global economic power had eroded.

As to levels of productivity, the manufacturing output per hour for 1975 to 1980 in American factories was lower than that of Canadian, French, German, Italian, Japanese, and British factories. The decline in productivity coincided with U.S. corporate investment in foreign operations and mergers rather than in improving the American industrial physical plant.

Looking at international trade over time also suggests performance problems for the American economy. In 1971 the U.S., for the first time in the twentieth century, suffered a trade deficit. President Nixon's devaluations of the dollar in 1971 and 1973 and the agreement to sell grain to the Soviet Union temporarily reversed the balance of payments dilemma of the United States but from 1974 through 1980 a trade surplus was recorded only in 1975. From 1970 to 1980, the dollar value of exports increased by $177.5 billion while imports increased by $200.8 billion (U.S. Department of Commerce, Bureau of the Census, 1981, p. 843). Exports as a percentage of GNP increased from 4.3% in 1970 to 8.5% in 1980. Imports as a percentage of GNP rose from 4 to 9.5% in the same period (*Dollars and Sense*, 1982, pp. 10–11).

An interesting and significant corollary to the declining trade advantage of the United States and the changes in the American economy was the continued growth in direct foreign investments in the 1970s. Between 1975 and 1978, the average increase per year was $13 billion and in 1979 and 1980 increases in annual foreign investment were $24.1 and 26.7 billion, respectively. By 1980, U.S. direct foreign investments had reached $213.5 billion (U.S. Department of Commerce, Bureau of the Census, 1981, p. 833). Data on corporate profits in Table 2.2 suggest that profits from foreign investment had risen from about 14% of corporate totals in the 1960s to 16% in the 1970s.

In particular, foreign shares of profits during recessionary periods (1973–1975 and 1979) rose relative to domestic profits. In addition, many multinational corporations derived one-third to one-half of their profits from foreign operations. Bluestone and Harrison (1982, p. 42) reported that by the late 1970s foreign profits accounted for one-third or more of the total profits of the 100 largest multinational corporations and banks.

The profits on foreign investments compensated for declining profits on domestic investments. Bluestone and Harrison reported on a study

Table 2.2. Corporate Profits 1960 to 1979: Domestic and Foreign

Year	All Industries (billion $)	Foreign Earned (billion $)	Foreign as Percentage of Total
1960	27.1	3.0	11%
1965	46.3	4.5	10
1970	41.3	6.5	16
1973	76.6	13.7	18
1974	85.1	16.3	19
1975	81.5	13.0	16
1976	102.5	14.3	14
1977	120.0	15.5	13
1978	140.3	19.7	14
1979	167.8	30.3	18

Source: Adapted from U.S. Department of Commerce, Bureau of the Census, *Statistical Abstract of the United States*, 1981, p. 552.

that asserted that inflation adjusted after-tax rates of profits of American corporations began to decline in the late 1960s and continued to lessen in the 1970s. Rates of profits of nonfinancial corporations in the United States fell from 15.5% between 1963–1966 to 12.7% during 1967–1970. The rate for the 1971–1974 period was 10.1%, and 9.7% for 1975–1978. Table 2.3, taken from Bluestone and Harrison, illustrates their own research on pre-tax profit rates in twelve industries from 1963 to 1975. As the table suggests, the average change in the rates of profits of all twelve industries across the time frame studied was −46.3%. Therefore, over the last two decades there were significant trends consisting of declining rates of profits, increased foreign investments, and increased profits on foreign operations as opposed to domestic operations. Such patterns document that the structure of the international political economy was of vital and growing importance to the sustenance of the largest corporations in America.

Turning to the domestic performance of the American economy, the impact on workers is especially significant. The American economy suffered from stagnation throughout the 1970s, with recessions in 1975 and the late 1970s. Soon after President Reagan assumed office, many economic indicators reached depression proportions. For example, the level of utilization of manufacturing capacity, which was up to 90% in the mid-1960s, averaged in the low 80% range in the 1970s and was down to 74.8% in the final quarter of 1981. Business failures, averaging

Table 2.3. Net Pre-Tax Profit Rates in Selected Manufacturing Industries: 1963–75[a]

Industry	1963–68 (%)	1969–75 (%)	Percentage Change
Rubber products	9.1	6.1	−36.2
Glass products	12.0	7.9	−34.2
Steel industry	7.3	4.4	−39.4
Fabricated metal products	8.0	6.4	−20.4
Radio, television equipment	12.2	3.8	−69.2
Machine products	13.9	9.3	−33.4
Farm machinery	8.4	4.1	−51.4
Machine tools	12.9	6.1	−53.1
Electrical equipment (heavy)	13.2	7.7	−49.1
Motor vehicles and parts	16.3	6.7	−64.8
Shipbuilding	5.8	3.1	−47.0
Railroad equipment	7.8	3.4	−56.9
Average (for the twelve industries)			−46.3

[a]Net profit rate = net pre-tax corporate income (less deficit) divided by total assets.
Source: Bluestone and Harrison, 1982, p. 148.

37 per 10,000 from 1970 to 1977, jumped from 24 per 10,000 businesses in 1978 to 83 per 10,000 in 1982. New housing construction peaking at 2,378,000 units started in 1972, dropped to less than a million units in 1982. In 1982, Leonard Silk reflected on the significance of these figures to the American economy. "Short term, it is obviously in a recession that started last fall; but this is the second recession since 1980, the third since 1975, and many economists believe that, even if recovery begins in the second half of this year, a fourth recession is just around the corner. It's been a long sequence of recessions and weak aborted expansions" (Silk, 1982, p. 1).

Magdoff and Sweezy (1981, p. 6) present graphs to show the declining rates of growth in industrial production in the 1970s as compared with extensions of trend lines from the 1960s. By 1980, an index score of industrial productivity was 50 points less than what 1960s trends would have predicted.

Because of strong foreign competition, foreign investment, lack of corporate investment in physical plant renovation, and often faulty de-

cision-making at the managerial level (e.g., automobile companies re-
fusing to produce small cars until foreign companies captured the market), major industrial sectors of the American economy, such as auto,
steel, and textiles, suffered from stagnation throughout the 1970s and
by the time of Reagan's election, had slipped deeper into crisis.

Capital Mobility, Unemployment, and Plant Closings

The impact of economic stagnation in the United States and Europe
had profoundly negative consequences on workers. Official unemployment rates in the U.S. ranged from 4.9 to 8.5% in the 1970s and by
December, 1982 had reached 10.8%. Even with modest economic recovery since 1982, unemployment rates remained about 7%. Blue-collar
workers experienced higher rates of unemployment than white-collar
workers, but even the latter were not immune from the results of economic crisis. The rates of unemployment among blacks and women
were at least double those of white men.

While much job loss was related to the general decline of American
economic dominance, unemployment was also a function of conscious
investment decisions. Major corporations, profitable in their traditional
operations, have been able to secure *more* profits by diversifying into
unrelated product or service lines. For example, *Business Week* (1979, p.
89) reported that U.S. Steel's "nonsteel assets grew 80% to $4.7 billion
during the past three years, while steel assets increased only 13% to
$5.9 billion." Frank and Freeman (1978, p. 156) found in 1970 that each
$1 billion of direct foreign investment eliminated 26,500 domestic jobs.
Corporations were investing in new and overseas ventures despite their
negative impacts on workers.

A dramatic manifestation of capital mobility is the escalating volume
of plant closings across the United States. Bluestone and Harrison (1982)
estimated that in the 1970s somewhere between 450,000 to 650,000 jobs
were lost as a result of "runaway shops" (movement of plant sites to
foreign countries). Further, "when the employment lost as a direct result of plant, store, and office *shutdowns* during the 1970s is added to
the job loss associated with runaway shops, it appears that more than
32 million jobs were destroyed. Together, runaways, shutdowns, and
permanent physical cutbacks short of complete closure may have cost
the country as many as 38 million jobs (Bluestone and Harrison, 1982,
p. 26)." Table 2.4 indicates the authors' estimates of the number of
plant closings occurring between 1969 and 1976 (over 100 employees).

Table 2.4. Selected Manufacturing Plants Open in 1969 and Closed by December 31, 1976[a]

Region	Number of States	Percentage of U.S. Population	Number of Plants in Sample	Number Closed by 1976	Proportion of 1969 Plants Closed	Percentage by Region
Northeast	9	24.1	4,576	1,437	.31	38.6
North Central	12	27.8	3,617	904	.25	24.2
South	16	31.0	3,101	1,042	.34	28.0
West	13	17.1	1,155	344	.30	9.2
Total	50	100.0	12,449	3,727	.30	100.0

[a]More than 100 employees.
Source: Bluestone and Harrison 1982, p. 32.

Of particular note is that 30% of the plants in existence in 1969 had closed by 1976. Also the proportion of the 1969 plants that closed in the South exceeded that for the Northeast and the North Central states.

Candee S. Harris (1984) reported on the intersection of recession, structural change in the economy, and plant closings. Unemployment due to the 1980 to 1982 recession exceeded that of the recessions of the 1970s and the percentage of permanent job losses in the most recent one exceeded the 1970s, 53 to 37%. She wrote that in 1982 there were 1.4 million fewer manufacturing jobs than in 1970.

> Closings of large firms eliminated over 16 million jobs between 1976 and 1982. Almost one-third of these were in the manufacturing sector. While small manufacturing firms—those with fewer than 100 employees—registered annual net employment growth rates around 6 percent between 1976 and 1982, larger firms contracted their employment. Rates of employment loss due to closings of manufacturing branches doubled in the 1980–82 period over the 1978–80 period, combining with lower replacement rates to produce a net decline of 5.2 percent in manufacturing (Harris, 1984, p. 26).

She adds that since 1976, plant closings have eliminated over 900,000 manufacturing jobs per year.

More recently (1986) the Office of Technology Assessment (OTA) of the U.S. Congress published a study entitled "Technology and Structural Unemployment: Reemploying Displaced Adults." They began their analysis of unemployment and plant closings by indicating that:

> In the past few years, millions of American workers have lost their jobs because of structural changes in the U.S. and world economies. Some of them—especially younger workers with skills in demand or the right educational background—have little trouble finding new jobs. Others—hundreds of thousands a year—remain out of work for many weeks or months, even for years. Many of the displaced are middle-aged unskilled or semiskilled manfacturing workers, with long and stable job histories (p.3).

The OTA study found that between 1979 and 1984, 11.5 million workers lost jobs because of plant shutdowns, relocations, and layoffs. Of these, 5.1 million had held their jobs for at least 3 years. By 1984, 1.3 million of those who had held their job for 3 years were still unemployed. At least one-half of those workers who found new jobs were earning less than they had before. Further, nearly one-half of those who lost jobs since 1979 had been in manufacturing employment. OTA estimated that between 1970 and 1984 nearly all new jobs created in the United States (94%) were in the service sector; only 1% were in manufacturing. Since 1979, manufacturing employment dropped by almost 1.5 million workers. For the most part, service sector jobs paid less than manufacturing jobs (Office of Technology Assessment, 1986, p. 11).

Other recent studies indicated possible byproducts of capital mobility, plant closings, and unemployment and suggested that the U.S. economy may be experiencing a significant shift in employment patterns. For example, Audrey Freedman, a labor economist at the Conference Board, noted a 25% increase in the number of temporary and part-time workers in the total work force between 1975 and 1985. By 1985 about 29.5 million of the 107 million U.S. workers were temporary or part-time employees (Serrin, 1986, p. 9).

Further, a joint Economic Committee of Congress study prepared by Bluestone and Harrison reported that over one-half of the eight million net new jobs created from 1979 to 1984 in the United States paid less than $7,000 a year. The authors of the report warned that the standard of living of a growing proportion of U.S. workers was being threatened. "The redesign of full-time into part-time jobs, the disproportionate growth of part-time or part-year work and the spread of wage freezes and concessions from one industry to another all suggest a decline in annual earnings" (*New York Times*, 1986, p. 18).

The increased joblessness, the threat of plant closings, and the emergence of a pool of low paid, part-time and temporary workers has facilitated corporate demands on unionized workers to make concessions on wages and benefits. A concessionary trend in labor-management negotiations has characterized the 1980s. For example, by 1985 the downward trend in wage gains in the private sector continued for the fourth straight year. First year wage increases in 1985 averaged 2.3%, the lowest figure since such factors were taken into account. The 1980s also witnessed a rise in lump-sum payments instead of wage increases (less costly to employers) and a steady rise in two-tier wage plans allowing a lower scale of wages for new workers. Of all contracts negotiated in 1983, 1984, and 1985, 29%, 27%, and 25%, respectively, called for wage freezes or cuts (*Economic Notes*, 1986, p. 1). Therefore, throughout the 1980s unions reluctantly agreed to concessions or "givebacks" on wages and benefits to forestall layoffs and plants closings.

Finally, Jaffee (1986) analyzed competing hypotheses relating to geographic shifts of manufacturing investment and jobs. One hypothesis linked capital mobility to various "industrial location" variables, such as proximity to retail markets, labor force training, cost of energy, and climate. Another hypothesis postulated a connection between capital mobility and "political–economic" explanations. He found that level of unionization was the best predictor of capital flight, such that in the 1970s corporations tended to move to states without powerful trade unions.

The analysis so far can be reduced to a series of summary statements. First, the U.S. economic dominance established after World War II was increasingly challenged by the rise in competitiveness of the Europeans and the Japanese. This relative decline in American economic dominance was clearly manifest by the 1970s.

Second, as a result of numerous forces, the rates of profit achieved by American corporations in the 1940s, 1950s, and 1960s were declining in the 1970s. The American economy was also experiencing declining rates of industrial productivity in the 1970s. Third, declining profit and productivity at home were coupled with increasing shares of profits being derived from foreign operations. Some of the world's largest corporations were deriving one-third or one-half of their total sales from foreign operations. Fourth, unemployment rates increased in the 1970s, reaching a postdepression peak in December, 1982 of 10.8%, and have continued a decline to about 7% since then. Declining production as well as the growing phenomena of plant closings led to layoffs of hundreds of thousands of workers. Workers securing new employment earned less than they did on their old jobs. Since the late 1970s more part-time and low-paying jobs have emerged. Finally, declining productivity, layoffs, and plant closings, forced the labor movement in the 1980s to begin to "give-back" the wages, fringes, and economic security it took years of struggle to achieve. Union contracts that reduced wages and cut fringe benefits, such as holidays and insurance, were reluctantly accepted by one union after another to forestall threats of more plant closings. The threat of factory shutdowns became a common negotiating tool for corporations.

The Transformation of the Electronics Industry

An examination of the electronics industry illustrates the interconnections between changes in the national economy, the international political economy, the production process, and the international division of labor. It also provides an understanding of the industrial sector which includes the television cabinets produced by RCA in Monticello, Indiana.

The changing historical context of electronics is reflected in a report on the industry prepared by the North American Congress on Latin America (NACLA). NACLA noted that the changes were part of a general process of globalization of production:

> Since the early 1960s production has taken a new turn, becoming increasingly internationalized in many industries. The structure which underlies this development is what one observer has called the "globally integrated manufacturing system." A single firm now integrates workers around the globe into one coordinated production system which reflects an international division of labor. Generally, workers in the United States labor at more capital-intensive, more highly skilled aspects of production while workers in Third World countries provide the labor-intensive, unskilled inputs. The product is one, whether it be a computer or a dress, but it directly reflects the labor of workers in several countries (NACLA, 1977b, p. 4).

Jeremy Brecher (1979) pointed out that the development and production of electrical products historically had gone through a pattern of research, production, and marketing based on capital mobility. When products were in the development stage, production facilities near major metropolitan centers and universities characterized the industry. When these developments led to mass production of consumer goods, production was dispersed to smaller cities and towns where lower wages could be paid. Before World War II 87% of electrical manufacturing was carried out in the nine states east of the Mississippi and north of the Mason-Dixon line. After the war, the major electrical companies carried out a planned expansion of facilities into the rural areas of the North and West, small towns in the South, and in suburban areas of large cities. Brecher quoted a General Electric executive who discussed some of the goals of plant relocations:

> From the labor relations point of view, this diversification is highly significant. It is clearly impossible to shut down this company by striking a key plant. . . . Moreover, in planning its general program of expansion during the last decade, GE has kept in view the employee relations aspect of plant operations and has built second or satellite plants in many cases where operations of a group of plants might be jeopardized by a strike in a sole supplying plant (Brecher, 1979, pp. 217–218).

Several features of the electronics industry facilitated the extensive capital mobility in the 1960s. The manufacturing process increasingly could be divisible into high technology and labor-intensive components, thus easing the movement of one sector to offshore plants. The high-priced components of electronics goods could be inexpensively shipped from Taiwan, South Korea or elsewhere because of their diminutive size. Further, U.S. tariff codes (Items 806.30 and 807) allowed for the reimportation of goods produced overseas with duties paid only on the value added, that is, the labor costs of workers in the Third World. In addition, since consumer goods in electronics were affected less by seasonal sales, corporations could afford to produce in plants far from retailers and markets.

Clearly, a central driving force for the export of jobs in the last 20 years has been cheap labor. Because of intense competition over prices in sectors of the electronics industry and dramatic new technological advances that often created new product lines, rates of profit could not as easily be maintained. Also investments in plant automation were impractical because product lines might be short-lived, hence plant obsolescence was a high probability. The answer to declining profit rates due to competition, new technologies, and union labor was to move plants overseas. Reducing the cost of wage labor became the major vehicle by which manufacturers tried to counter the tendencies for declining profit rates. *NACLA* data on average hourly wages for unskilled workers in Asia in 1976 describes the wage patterns that encouraged the shift of electronics, indeed all manufacturing, overseas.

Between 1965 and 1975 the electronics industry grew dramatically but domestic employment in the industry did not keep pace with this

Table 2.5. Average Hourly Wage in Asia

Country	Hourly Wage ($)
Indonesia	.17
Thailand	.26
Philippines	.32
India	.37
Taiwan	.37
Malaysia	.41
South Korea	.52
Hong Kong	.55
Singapore	.62

Source: NACLA, April, 1977a, p. 15.

Table 2.6. Value of Electronics Products Imported into the U.S.
Under Items 806.30 and 807.00, 1966 and 1975
(Thousands of U.S. Dollars)

Product Description	1966 ($)	1975 ($)
Television receivers	9,515	103,379
Television apparatus and parts	26,041	287,736
Radio apparatus and parts	11,904	133,690
Phonographs and parts	11,083	31,051
Semiconductors and parts	51,584	617,499
Electronic memories	12,373	927,415
Consumer electronics products and parts		8,700
Total	122,500	2,109,470

Source: NACLA, April, 1977a, p. 12.

growth for two reasons. First, during this period there was a movement of plants overseas and, second, technological advances increased
the productivity of American workers. In the production of radios and
television sets domestic employment between 1967 and 1977 declined
by 250,000. Overtime work in the 1970s declined by 50% over the 1960s.
To give some sense of the magnitude of the impacts of runaway shops,
Table 2.6 illustrates the dollar value of electronics goods imported under the favorable tariff code provisions referred to above. By 1975, 70%
of all electronics imports entered the United States under these codes,
and electronics constituted 15% of all goods entering the United States
under the 806/807 provisions. Between 1966 and 1975 electronics sales
doubled in the United States while offshore production increased ten
times.

Finally, Table 2.7 indicates some of the major sites for U.S. plants in
foreign countries in the electronics field. With the possible exceptions
of India and Jamaica (from 1972 to 1980), all the countries on the list
had close ties with the United States. Some, like El Salvador, the Do-
minican Republic, Haiti, Taiwan, South Korea, the Philippines, Thai-
land, Indonesia, and Spain, had histories of civilian or military dicta-
torship which, in the short run, created stable economic climates. In
most cases, trade unions were weak, nonexistent, or extensions of the
governmental apparatus designed to control a docile work force.

A recent *New York Times* article (Blumstein, 1983) described the his-

Table 2.7. U.S. Electronics Plants by Region (Number of Plants)

Latin America	Number	Asia	Number	Europe	Number
Mexico	193	Hong Kong	45	Spain	29
Puerto Rico	140	Taiwan	45	Ireland	22
Jamaica	9	India	32	Scotland	18
Barbados	5	Singapore	30	Portugal	14
El Salvador	5	Malaysia	23	Malta	1
Dominican Republic	4	South Korea	19		
Trinidad & Tobago	4	Philippines	17		
Curacao	3	Thailand	8		
Haiti	3	Indonesia	6		
Bermuda	2	Okinawa	1		
Virgin Islands	2				

Source: NACLA, April, 1977a, p. 13.

torical evolution of one electronics manufacturer, Zenith. A major domestic producer of radios and then television sets, Zenith began to
publicly complain about Japanese competition in 1968. By the late 1970s,
Zenith had been superseded by RCA, which used price-cutting tech-
niques to become the leading domestic television distributor.

Under new leadership at Zenith, Blumstein reported . . . "the company tried to compete by lowering its costs and expanding its product
line into related but potentially more profitable areas." Blumstein quoted
from a Merrill Lynch financial analyst, who said, "They finally realized
that you don't win the war in Washington; you fight the battle in the
plants to get costs down."

With cost-cutting as the key to increased profit, Zenith moved their
manufacturing facilities for black and white television sets to Taiwan
and for color television components and modules to Mexico. Concom-
itantly with the runaway shops, Zenith sold several "obsolete" color
television assembly plants in Chicago and built an automated plant in
Springfield, Missouri. Zenith also invested in new product lines including various computer products. Finally, they purchased an electronics
do-it-yourself kit-making company. While Blumstein did not dwell
on the subject, it is clear that if Zenith was to regain its financial integ-
rity it would result in good measure from the cheap labor of those
workers in Taiwan and Mexico and at the expense of the workers of
Chicago and elsewhere that were left jobless by the movement of manufacturing facilities to other countries.

A cursory examination of the electronics industry suggests that over the past 30 years its nature, size, location, and costs of production have changed. The internationalization of its production paralleled the internationalization of American capitalism. The drive for cheaper labor, in conjunction with increased foreign competition and declining profit rates stimulated the movement of production sites away from the industrial heartland of the United States to the South and West and, ultimately, to the Third World. The experiences of this industrial sector provides a model of the change in the American economy that bears directly on plant closings and unemployment.

A Portrait of RCA

RCA was incorporated in 1919 as a result of encouragement from the federal government, General Electric, and the American Telephone and Telegraph Company. It was established to provide another corporate vehicle for developing and keeping electronic technology in the United States. One stem of the RCA corporate tree was the purchase of the British-owned Marconi Wireless Telegraph Company. A wireless operator for Marconi, David Sarnoff, stayed on as the new company was formed and eventually became its chief executive officer in the 1930s. RCA was a pioneer in the mass production of radios and developed the first television set, which was displayed at the 1939 World's Fair. They marketed their first black and white television sets in 1946. The company developed color television in 1950. Since the 1970s, RCA had become a conglomerate or what *Forbes* refers to as "multi-industry companies." For a time it owned a frozen chicken company and a book publisher. By the 1980s it engaged in electronics, broadcasting, financial services, communications technology, and automobile rentals.

Although RCA became a conglomerate in the 1970s, consumer electronics still constituted one-third to one-half of RCA sales in the 1980s. It led in sales of color TV sets within the United States, selling one of five in 1979. Most of RCA's production facilities for TVs were in the United States, but some were manufactured in Canada, Taiwan, and Mexico. In addition, RCA has a global communication service, two communications satellites, and, of course, is actively engaged in broadcasting.

Aside from electronics, communications, and broadcasting, RCA gained substantial profits from Hertz Rent-A-Car, a company that in 1979 held 40% of the car rental market. Finally, RCA bought C.I.T. Financial, in 1978, a financial and insurance company with many subsidiaries of its own. Major portions of C.I.T. were sold to Manufacturers Hanover for $1.5 billion in 1983. RCA's financial and geographic dispersal in 1979 is illustrated by the following:

RCA owns 15.8 million square feet of the 65 plants they operate in the United States and abroad. Their plants are located in Indiana, Ohio, Pennsylvania, New Jersey, Massachusetts, Illinois, California, Missouri, Arkansas, and Georgia—a total of 47 in the United States—as well as Malaysia, Taiwan, Ontario, United Kingdom, Brazil, and Mexico. They own nine TV and radio stations in New York, San Francisco, Los Angeles, Chicago, Cleveland, and Washington, D.C. Antenna fields are located in Alaska, Florida, Louisiana, and other coastal areas. RCA owns 90 of the 1,500 Hertz offices around the country. The David Sarnoff research center occupies a 342-acre tract of land in Princeton, New Jersey (Moskowitz *et al.*, 1980, pp. 844–845).

The diversification of the 1970s, the business press argued, was the source of problems for RCA. *Business Week* reported in August 17, 1981, that RCA profits came heavily from car rentals and financial services, at the expense of traditional product lines. The purchases of C.I.T. and other companies created high indebtedness for the company. *Fortune* noted in 1982 that over the prior 3 years debt had nearly doubled to $2.9 billion.

The most critical factor in the problematic RCA earnings record was that 1981 profits plummeted 82.9% from the 1980 figure, the second largest decline in its 63-year history. Net income for 1979 and 1980 was $283.8 million and $315.3 million, respectively. In 1981, net income dropped to $54 million. Figures for 1982 and 1983 rose to $222.6 and $240.8 million, respectively. During these years, RCA employment dropped from 133,000 in 1980, to 119,000 in 1981, 109,000 in 1982, and 110,000 in 1983 (RCA, Annual Report, 1983, pp. 39, 46). "The major causes for the poor 1981 earnings, according to RCA, were increased costs of carrying its debt and a substantial write-off of unproductive properties" (Friedman, 1982, p. 1).

As a result of 6 years of shuffling of executive officers in the company, dubious expansion into areas aside from electronics, high debt, declining consumer electronics sales due to recession, poor sales of the new video disc product line, and the poor profit performance in 1981, RCA corporation chairman, Thornton Bradshaw, stated in early 1982 that RCA would begin to restructure the corporation to return to its traditional businesses—electronics, communications, and broadcasting (*Fortune*, March 22, 1982).

Table 2.8. *Forbes* **Ranking of RCA, 1981, 1982, 1983** [a]

Year	Assets	Sales	Market Value	Net Profits
1981	51	51	162	x[b]
1982	57	45	139	120
1983	127	53	119	135

[a] Rank number among top 500 corporations.
[b] Not on top 500 list, 1981.
Sources: Forbes, 1984, 1983, 1982.

Table 2.8 suggests the impact of chairman Bradshaw's new policies. Between 1981 and 1982, RCA's ranking among all corporations worsened in assets but improved in sales, market value, and net profits (1983 rankings were worse than 1982 in assets, sales, and net profits and better in market value). This data along with net income figures suggests that 1982 was a year of relative economic recovery for the company. (Even though RCA's relative rankings worsened in 1983 over 1982, profits continued to climb in the former year.) Chairman Thornton F. Bradshaw reported:

> RCA had a good year in 1982 despite the severe recession. We are encouraged by the company's progress in general and with the improvement in our financial condition. The fourth quarter results reflect a continuation of the weak economy, which may carry over into the first quarter of this year. Nonetheless, our operations are positioned to make further progress in 1983 with some help from an improved economy. (*RCA Quarterly Review for Shareholders*, Fourth Quarter, 1982)

After the peak years of 1978, 1979, and 1980 and the dramatic decline of 1981, RCA improved its profit totals in 1982 and 1983. Further, RCA remained the number one U.S. producer of television sets for domestic sales. In 1983, the Consumer Products and Services subsegment had a sales increase of 13% and a profit increase of 35%, led by substantially higher unit sales of color television sets, particularly in the larger screen sizes, and video cassette recorders (*RCA 1983 Annual Report*, p. 311).

In sum, the business press suggested that RCA, from the late 1970s until 1982, was a company experimenting with diversification that suffered a major profit decline (by its standards) in 1981. The profit "crash" of 1981 was followed by recoveries in 1982 and 1983. Despite purchases of other firms, RCA maintained a strong commitment to consumer electronics and remained the preeminent American producer of television sets. What can be concluded from the data is that RCA had suffered short-term losses but was not in severe financial danger. RCA profits were probably a temporary victim of the recession of 1980 and 1981. Closing union plants and moving to cheaper labor sources was one way to increase profit rates. However, RCA net income for 1982 was four times greater than 1981. Since the RCA television cabinet plant in Monticello, Indiana did not close until December, 1982, the need for increased profits did not require closing the plant in question.

The Economy of the Midwest

Corporations have moved from place to place in the continual search for expanded profits. The "push" to mobility involved declining profit rates, which stimulated a reconsideration of the location of corporate activities and the very desirability of continuing to produce goods traditional to the company. The "pull" of corporations has been cheap labor in the Third World and non-union areas of the United States. As to the latter, Goodman (1979, p. 41) reported:

> Between 1970 and 1978, the least unionized states as a whole added double the number of jobs for each of their residents than did the most unionized ones; during the same period the ten least unionized states as a whole added more than triple the number of jobs for each of their residents than did the ten most unionized states.

The "pushes" and "pulls" of the last 15 years led gradually to the restructuring of the industrial base of the Midwest. *Congressional Quarterly* (1983) reported that economic growth in the Great Lakes states (Wisconsin, Illinois, Indiana, Michigan, and Ohio) since World War II was far below other regions of the country. From 1950 to 1975, manufacturing employment in the area rose by 4.3% compared to 76% in the Southeast and 141% in the Southwest.

By the 1970s deindustrialization in the Midwest impacted dramatically on steel and automobile production, the region's two primary industrial sectors. U.S. steel production had peaked at 111.4 million tons in 1973 and dropped to 97.9 million tons by 1978. By the 1980s, steel imports constituted over 26% of the amount sold in the United States. Declining production, mostly in the Midwest, and imports led to 100,000 steel jobs being lost between 1960 and 1980. By 1982, steel jobs were down 36% compared to 1976 (*Congressional Quarterly*, 1983, p. 179).

**Table 2.9. Unemployment Rates
1974–1983**[a]

Year	U.S.	Region[b]
1974	5.6	5.3
1975	8.5	10.8
1976	7.7	7.5
1977	7.1	6.7
1978	6.1	6.0
1979	5.8	6.3
1980	7.1	9.5
1981	7.6	9.9
1982 August	9.6	12.4
1983	9.5	10.1[c]

[a]Percentage of work force.
[b]Region includes: Indiana, Illinois, Ohio, Michigan, and Wisconsin.
[c]Fourth quarter, 1983.
Source: Fitzgerald (1982, p. 4); Stamas, September, 1984, p. 12; *Monthly Labor Review*, February, 1984, p. 73.

American automobile manufacturers lost $4.2 billion in 1980 and $1.8 billion in 1981. Some companies like Chrysler and American Motors were near bankruptcy during this period. While profits returned to the industry by 1982, temporary and permanent unemployment in the industry remained high. By March, 1983, 300,000 automobile workers had been laid-off, most never to return to work (*Congressional Quarterly*, 1983).

Comparing U.S. average unemployment rates with the five Great Lakes states (Indiana, Illinois, Ohio, Michigan, and Wisconsin) from 1974 to 1983 suggests some interesting patterns. From 1974 to 1978, U.S. unemployment rates exceeded the five states, except for 1975 (see Table 2.9). During the 1975 recession, the rate of unemployment for the nation was 8.5%, the five-state region 10.8%. However, from 1979 onward, the region's unemployment exceeded that of the national average. In other words, the industrial manufacturing sectors so vital to the economies of midwestern states were exceedingly sensitive to recessionary pressures.

Finally, the Office of Technology Assessment (1986) reported that as of 1984 the Great Lakes states had 400,000 displaced workers, defined as those serving in a job for at least 3 years, who lost their job between

January, 1979 and January, 1984 because of plant closings, layoffs, and ending whole shifts of workers. The total number of displaced workers nationally was 1,299,000 so that about 30% of those displaced came from five Midwestern states.

The Economy of Indiana

Throughout the postwar period, Indiana, the site of the plant closing of our study, had a strong, but declining, industrial base. Its principal manufacturing goods included metals, transportation equipment, electrical and electronic equipment, and processed foods. In 1974, 36.3% of the work force was in manufacturing; in 1980 31%; in 1984, 29% (Indiana Employment Security Division, 1985).

Table 2.10 indicates that unemployment in Indiana began to rise in 1979. Comparing Indiana figures with the five-state region in Table 2.9, Indiana exceeded regional averages in 1979, 1980, and 1981. Indiana also continued to exceed national rates of unemployment from 1982 onward. Table 2.11 shows that the changing character of the economy meant a net loss of manufacturing jobs in key sectors of the Indiana economy, with gains reported in nonmanufacturing and service.

Table 2.12 illustrates that as the recession worsened after 1979, substantial job loss began to occur in both manufacturing and service in a short period of time, with jobs lost in 14 of the 15 categories listed. In

Table 2.10. Indiana Unemployment Rates

Year	Labor Force	Unemployed	Rate (%)
1976	2,438,000	148,000	6.1
1977	2,468,000	141,000	5.7
1978	2,577,000	146,000	5.7
1979	2,610,000	167,000	6.4
1980	2,620,000	253,000	9.6
1981	2,627,000	264,000	10.0
1982	2,594,000	310,000	12.0
1983	2,584,000	286,000	11.1
1984	2,621,000	226,000	8.5
1985	2,735,000	215,000	7.9

Source: Indiana Employment Security Division, 1976–1985.

Table 2.11. Indiana Employment by Selected Sectors 1973–1980

Sector	1973	1980	Jobs Lost
Manufacturing			
Lumber and wood products	25,100	18,800	−6,300
Furniture	24,200	19,300	−4,900
Stone, clay, glass	25,900	21,600	−4,300
Primary metals	111,900	101,600	−10,300
Fabricated metals	69,700	54,700	−15,000
Nonelectrical machinery	76,000	74,800	−1,200
Electrical machinery	136,300	102,000	−34,300
Transportation equipment	101,200	83,400	−17,800
Apparel and textiles	14,800	11,200	−3,600
Rubber and plastic products	34,800	31,100	−3,700
Nonmanufacturing			
Contract construction	90,500	91,600	+1,100
Transporation, communication, utilities	104,600	105,000	+400
Wholesale, retail trade	418,200	478,200	+60,000
Finance, insurance, real estate	48,500	101,900	+17,400
Services	261,300	337,100	+53,400

Source: Indiana Employment Security Division, 1981.

the period from 1977 (before the onset of the recent recession) to 1980 manufacturing employment in Indiana dropped from 713,200 to 658,000, a loss of 55,200 jobs. Job loss was experienced throughout the state (Clark, 1981, p. 2).

The Indiana Citizens Action Coalition (CAC) reported that 25,000 of the jobs lost between 1977 and 1980 were lost because of 160 plant shutdowns in Indiana (Clark, 1981). Consequently, between 1977 and 1980, 45% of the jobs lost in Indiana were caused by the direct effects of plant closings. If "ripple effects" are added to the direct job loss from plant closings, the latter could be seen to impact dramatically on unemployment rates. Table 2.13 provides a partial list of plant closings in Indiana from 1975 to 1983, which includes the CAC data. During this time frame there were at least 208 closings and 37,691 workers dislocated.

Charles Craypo (1984) documented the patterns of plant closings and

Table 2.12. Indiana Employment by Selected Sectors, 1980–1981

Sector	January 1980 (employed)	January 1981 (employed)	Jobs Lost
Lumber and wood products	19,100	18,100	−1,000
Furniture	20,200	19,200	−1,000
Stone, clay, glass	22,800	21,000	−1,800
Primary metals	107,100	102,300	−4,800
Fabricated metals	59,400	54,100	−5,300
Nonelectrical machinery	81,500	72,900	−8,600
Electrical machinery	109,800	105,600	−4,200
Transporation equipment	84,800	83,500	−1,300
Apparel and textiles	11,100	10,500	−600
Rubber and plastic products	33,800	31,400	−2,400
Contract construction	88,500	79,600	−8,900
Transportation, communication, utilities	108,100	100,500	−7,600
Wholesale, retail trade	478,600	468,000	−10,600
Finance, insurance, real estate	101,000	101,300	+300
Services	329,500	323,900	−5,600

Source: Indiana Employment Security Division, 1981.

layoffs in the South Bend-Mishawaka area of Northeast Indiana from 1954 to 1983. He identified 27 plant closings in this period affecting 14,716 workers at the time of closing. Since most employers cut back their work force before closing, Craypo also gathered data on the "historical peak number of employees," and discovered that 37,150 workers lost jobs in the 27 plants analyzed. Table 2.14 shows changes in 30 years among the eight largest manufacturers in the area. Thirty-four thousand jobs were lost and three factories closed during this period. Finally, Table 2.15 illustrates the plant closing phenomena in the midnorth Indiana area around Lafayette (and including Monticello). Therefore, available data suggest that plant closings blanketed the state from 1975 onward, with shutdowns experienced in at least 53 of Indiana's 103 counties (Clark, 1981).

Table 2.13. Partial List of Indiana Plant Closings, 1975–1983

Year	Number of Closings	Workers Affected
1975	9	1,785
1976	NA	NA
1977	14	535
1978	34	7,944
1979	32	4,763
1980	82	11,433
1981	NA	NA
1982	21	11,231
1983	16	NA
	208	37,691

Source: For 1975–1980 Clark, "Report on Indiana Plant Closings Job Loss, "unpublished manuscript, Citizens Action Coalition, 1981; for 1982 and 1983, The Bureau of National Affairs, 1983, 1984.

Table 2.14. Employment Changes Between 1953 and 1983 in the Eight Largest South Bend-Mishawaka Manufacturers

	Average Employment		
Company	1953	April, 1983	Net Change
Studebaker	20,524	Closed	−20,524
Bendix	11,762	5,700	−6,062
Uniroyal	5,300	1,130	−4,170
White Farm	1,500	100	−1,400
Singer	1,500	Closed	−1,500
Wheelabrator-Frye	900	493	−407
Dodge-Reliance-Exxon	900	534	−366
Wilson Bros.	750	Closed	−750
Total	43,136	7,957	34,179

Source: Craypo, 1984, p. 31.

Table 2.15. Plant Closings in North Central Indiana 1977–1983 [a]

Plant	City	Year Closed	Number Displaced
U.S. Metalite	Lafayette	1977	25
Coin Accepters	Lafayette	1977	90
Revington and Co.	Lafayette	1977	35
Dean Foods	Lafayette	1977	25
Jules Simon	Frankfort	1977	100
Graves Bakery	Lafayette	1977	50
Formica Corp.	Frankfort	1979	94
Peerless Wire	Lafayette	1979	152
Essex Wire	Lafayette	1979	184
ECC Corp.	Lafayette	1979	30
Wilderness Indus.	Frankfort	1979/80 (uncertain)	125
Igram-Richardson	Frankfort	1979/80 (uncertain)	75
Bryan Manuf.	Monticello	1980	160
Essex Int'l.	Fowler	1980	105
Carr Cabinet	Frankfort	1980 (uncertain)	45
Del Monte Corp.	Frankfort	1981	300
New Century Homes	Lafayette	1982	70
RCA Corporation	Monticello	1982	1,200
Kroger	Lafayette	1983	150
Woolco	Lafayette	1983	80
Montomery Ward	Lafayette	1983	185
Cadbury	Frankfort	1983	220
Total	22 Closings		3,500 Workers displaced

[a]This is a very incomplete list of closings. Data on plant closings is, in any case, fragmentary and difficult to obtain. Sources for the information include the Indiana Employment Security Division.

A Profile of White County, Indiana, and Monticello

Monticello, a city of 5,160 people, is in White County (23,737 population) in northwest Indiana. Monticello was chartered in 1834 and has been the county seat and commercial center of White County ever since. On April 3, 1974, a tornado destroyed much of Monticello's downtown business section, causing $100 million in damage and eight deaths. After the tornado, a major renovation of the center of town was completed.

The major forms of business in White County since 1970 are listed in Table 2.16. The table identifies business activities that reflect high or low growth in employment in the county and high or low business stability in employment. Stability was defined as the level of steady employment compared with statewide employment/business cycle fluctuations (Brown *et al.*, 1983). The less the county employment was affected by general statewide economic trends, the more stable its business climate was understood to be. Table 2.17 identifies the major employment sectors in White County for September 1970 and September 1982. The data were gathered for each standard industrial classification having at least 100 employees.

These tables indicate that transportation equipment (Monon Trailer Company in Monon, Indiana) and furniture manufacturing (RCA in Monticello) were among the high growth and most stable businesses in the county. Amusement, recreation, restaurants, and bars constituted a high growth but low stable business component of the county economy. The Monticello area is a major tourist center with an amusement park, two lakes, and dining and lodging facilities.

In 1970, according to Table 2.17, 28% of the total standard industrial classification employees tabulated in White County were engaged in furniture manufacturing, 19% in electrical machinery, and 15% in eating and drinking establishments. The figures reflected the importance of the RCA television cabinet-making plant in 1970 as well as electrical machinery and tourism. In 1982 (even before the plant closing at RCA), furniture manufacturing had declined to 10% of the larger standard

Table 2.16. Business Stability and Growth in White County, 1970–1980

Stability	High Growth	Low Growth
High	Furniture manufacturing	Miscellaneous retail
	Nonelectrical machinery manufacturing	Wholesale trade: nondurables
	Communication	Utilities
	Banking	
	Trucking and warehousing (including grain storage)	
Low	Amusement and recreation	Food stores
	Eating and drinking places	Building material stores
	General merchandise stores	

Sources: Smith, 1984; Brown *et al.*, 1983.

Table 2.17. Employees by Standard Industrial Classification (SIC), White County, 1970, 1982[a]

SIC	Number Employed	
	September, 1970	September, 1982
Agriculture (laborers)	0	113
Furniture manufacturing	702	493
Rubber and plastic manufacturing	0	182
Non-electrical machinery	0	275
Electrical machinery	485	165
Transportation equipment	127	762
Trucking and warehousing	0	204
Communication	140	111
Electric, gas and sanitary services	171	169
Wholesale trade		
Durables	113	120
Nondurables	0	216
General merchandise stores	0	105
Food stores	140	199
Auto stores and service stations	141	259
Eating and drinking places	389	606
Miscellaneous retail	130	198
Banking	0	139
Hotels and lodging places	0	127
Amusement and recreation	0	420
Health services	0	161

[a]Figures show employment in September 1970 and September, 1982 for all two-digit standard industrial code classification sectors which employed 100 or more employees in the county as of September, 1982.

Source: Brown *et al.*, 1983, p. 171.

industrial classification totals but furniture manufacturing still accounted for a little over 25% of White County's manufacturing employment. Tourism (reflected in eating and drinking places, amusement, recreation, hotels, and lodging) rose to 23% of the total. The number of employees engaged in producing transportation equipment increased dramatically from 1970 to 1982 to constitute 40% of White County manufacturing employment and 15% of all employment.

Table 2.18 indicates that approximately one-fourth of all employment in White County (business, government, agriculture, manufactur-

Table 2.18. Manufacturing Employment in White County, 1967–1982 (Alternate Years)

Year	Number of Employees	Percentage of Total Employment
1967	2,142	25.55
1968	2,529	28.73
1970	1,899	22.90
1972	2,393	26.93
1974	2,437	25.86
1976	2,483	25.18
1978	2,797	27.10
1980	2,664	25.52
1982	2,261	NA[a]

[a]NA, not available.
Source: INDIRS, 1984.

ing, retail trade etc.) over the past 15 years has been in manufacturing. In typical years, furniture manufacturing constituted between one-fourth and one-third of the total manufacturing employment.

As Table 2.19 suggests, patterns of unemployment paralleled developments in the Midwest and Indiana as a whole, with some variation. In 1976, 1980, and 1981, Indiana's percentage unemployed exceeded

Table 2.19. Unemployment in White County, 1974–1984 (Annual Averages)

Year	Number Unemployed	Unemployment Rate (county)
1974	430[a]	4.6[a]
1976	570[a]	5.9[a]
1978	787[a]	7.7[a]
1980	1,000	8.9
1981	1,125	9.8
1982	1,540	13.7
1983	1,740	15.4
1984	1,770[a]	16.1[a]

[a]January data.
Source: Indiana Employment Security Division, 1974–1985.

the county; in 1978, 1982, and 1983 the county unemployment was higher than the state average.

As of March, 1982, the Monticello, Indiana area had thirteen industries employing 1,294 people. Of these, 748 were men and 546 women. Company sizes ranged from a concrete block company with two employees to the RCA plant employing 692 (some RCA workers beyond this number were already on extended layoff) (Monticello Chamber of Commerce, 1982).

In sum, the White County economy had been dominated by manufacturing, retail trade (much of which is tied to tourism), and farming. While Indiana manufacturing employment had experienced decline in the 1970s and early 1980s, White County manufacturing employment did not vary in a consistent downward trend (Table 2.18). As of 1982, RCA was the largest employer in Monticello, the second in the county (Monon Trailer Company was first). Given the relatively large manufacturing work force for a small rural county, impacts of a large plant closing would inevitably reverberate throughout the city and county in which the plant had existed.

From the Global Political Economy to Monticello, Indiana

This chapter began with a survey of the changing character of the global political economy since World War II. Drawing upon Bluestone and Harrison's groundbreaking analysis, capital flight in pursuit of greater profits through cheap labor was examined. These authors argued that one significant byproduct of capital flight has been a tendency for a declining U.S. industrial base.

Many indicators suggest that the region of the nation hardest hit by deindustrialization has been the Midwest. With an industrial base evidencing less growth even before the waves of deindustrialization beginning in the 1960s, the Midwest was significantly impacted by capital flight by the 1970s, particularly during periods of national recession. The Great Lakes states (Illinois, Indiana, Michigan, Ohio, Wisconsin) in recent years experienced unemployment rates exceeding national averages. The state of Indiana witnessed unemployment rates and frequencies of plant closings parallel to the experiences of the other states in the region.

Finally White County and Monticello, Indiana experienced variations in levels of manufacturing employment in the 1970s and 1980s before the RCA plant closing but no clear downward trend was noted.

As will be examined later, the impact of the closing on the social and economic environment in Monticello was substantial.

Given the trends outlined above it seems clear that the patterns of capital mobility established at the global level in the 1960s were inextricably tied to the transformations of the national economy and its varied regions. With the Midwest starkly impacted by capital flight, local communities such as Monticello, Indiana were likely to experience their own capital flight as time progressed. To this degree, therefore, the RCA plant closing in Monticello, Indiana is part of a global political and economic process of capital accumulation and profit maximization characteristic of the historical epoch beginning after World War II, and continuing today.

3

COMMUNITY AND WORKER RESPONSES
TO A PLANT CLOSING

Assessing the Impacts of a Plant Closing

A plant closing is a public event that affects the workers immediately displaced and the larger community in which the plant is located. Businesses and their employees may experience declining consumer demand and job layoffs due to reduced sales. Charitable organizations, which were the beneficiaries of worker and corporate generosity, may suffer declining donations. Social agencies such as the welfare department and the unemployment agency may experience excess demand on services at a time when resources to administer public programs are cut. Also the community may experience increased death rates, incidences of child abuse, and other increases in aggregate physical and emotional responses to the closing. These are all aggregate effects on a community and work force that will be examined in this chapter. Subsequent chapters will examine the effects of closings on the physical and psychological health of the displaced workers and their political understanding of the closing experience.

Before discussing the closing it is important to suggest that a distinction be drawn between measurable impacts of a closing and perceived impacts. In some cases, actors in the community setting who were interviewed overestimated or underestimated the impacts of the closing on the workers and their community. Comparisons of "actual" and perceived impacts will be noted in the text. At this stage it is suggested that both kinds of data, even if at variance from each other, constitute critical elements of a plant closing context. Overestimates of food stamp use or underestimates of house foreclosures affect how community members act to overcome the impacts of the closing. Further, overestimates of effects and dire predictions increase the stress levels of public officials, citizens of the community, and workers and their families as all try to cope with a plant closing. Hence perceptions of impacts constitute a kind of impact on workers and their communities.

RCA and United Brotherhood of Carpenters and Joiners Local #3154 in Monticello: The Closing

The Monticello RCA plant was established in 1946 when the company purchased the site on Hanawalt Street in a residential neighborhood from the Monticello Cabinet Company. The plant was originally built in 1910. In the early 1960s, RCA almost doubled the plant size allowing for an increase of the work force from 600 to 1200 employees. In the middle 1960s, about 37% of all color television sets used furniture cabinets and since RCA has been a leader in their U.S. production, the Monticello plant played a major role in RCA television production. In the late 1970s, RCA built another cabinet plant in North Carolina, but the work force was not unionized. Periodically, executives from the Monticello plant would be transferred to the newer facility.

Unionization came to the Monticello Cabinet Company in 1937 with the formation of a carpenters' local. In 1943, the United Brotherhood of Carpenters and Joiners Local 3154 was chartered. It remained as the official bargaining agent of the workers when RCA purchased the plant in 1946. Local 3154 owned a union hall about four blocks from the factory and in the 1960s had 1200 members. Through reduced production and layoffs the local membership dropped to about 650 in the early 1980s. The union hall was the site of social events as well as business meetings. In recent years, the only regular social events were an annual picnic, which would draw virtually the entire membership in attendance, and a Christmas party for children of members. Bimonthly business meetings would usually draw from 30 to 50 people.

In March 1982 two hundred RCA workers were laid off indefinitely leaving about 450 still working. Spokespersons for the company said the layoffs resulted from reduced sales expectations for large screen color television sets in wood cabinets. The RCA plant was also closed for two weeks in March for "inventory adjustment." The RCA official said: "Industry sales of color television receivers have slowed down in the first quarter and industry factory inventories are presently 46 percent above the same period last year" (*Monticello Herald Journal*, March 1, 1982).

Three months later, local RCA company officials issued a warning to union leaders that workers must reduce the cost of manufacturing television cabinets or face the possibility of the plant closing. The *Herald Journal*, the local newspaper, noted that the Monticello plant was working an 8-hour 5-day week producing 5750 large console television cabinets each week. At the time of the warning about 400 hourly workers and 50 salaried employees remained on the payroll.

RCA officials above the plant level claimed that "cash flow and foreign competition" were the basis of the warning and that ". . . the current recessionary economic climate is a definite negative consideration in the highly competitive television receiver industry which is under severe cost and price pressures." Increased television imports from the Far East ". . . has aggravated the situation and increased these pressures on domestic manufacturers." The company also claimed that consumer preferences had ". . . changed significantly" leading to "increased demand" for smaller, more compact sets in plastic cabinets (McDonough, June 7, 1982a).

The United Brotherhood of Carpenters and Joiners Local 3154 local president, union stewards, and local company officials met with the work force to communicate RCA's warning. The union president said; "There is a probability that the factory will close. We must get the cost out of manufacturing the television cabinets but we have to keep quality." He noted that the UBCJ contract would expire in December, 1982, which gives ". . . but a short time to begin manufacturing less expensive television cabinets." He concluded: "The union will do whatever is necessary to get the cost down and keep the plant open. The Monticello plant has to remain open" (McDonough, June 7, 1982a).

The union president said that after the RCA warning he began to ask for clarification of the statement. After unclear responses from the company, RCA agreed to meet in July, 1982 with a seven-person negotiating team which could presumably negotiate new contracts or a closing agreement. The negotiating team included a regional representative from the United Brotherhood of Carpenters and Joiners and for a short time was aided by a lawyer provided by the union. The union president said of the negotiations:

> Overall, I'd say we met with them a lot of times and couldn't get an answer until we filed charges with the labor board. Then they did sit down and talk to us, and that's when we met in Indianap-

olis to negotiate and after the first day you knew that there was nothing you could do, but we had to do what you could, and they were polite to us. They gave us any information we wanted and anything we'd ask for they'd have the next day for us. They weren't being uncooperative—they just didn't want to keep the factory open.

The president reported that the first week of negotiations with RCA (presumably over contract terms for after the December 1982 contract expiration date) was spent on being informed by management about RCA's financial position. RCA officials claimed that sales on large cabinets had been declining and ". . . they got people they pay to see what's going to happen five years from now and they had that written out and wages were completely out of perspective. Of course, we offered to give half of them back but it wasn't good enough." He said RCA told the negotiating team of the costs to repair the factory roof and of increased maintenance costs. They told of RCA's huge costs for film rights for their video discs. Management spoke also of prior plans to close the plant in 1981 and of the impacts of the recessionary economy.

The president asked what guarantees there would be, if the workers made major concessions, that the plant would be open in 3 years. RCA said none. Despite the fact that the workers knew that concessions would not guarantee long-term employment, the negotiating team offered a package of extensive concessions. At first, the negotiating team offered a 10% cut in wages. RCA rejected the proposal. It was followed with a concession package that included an 18% wage cut and substantial givebacks including two sick days, two holidays, and the employee dental plan. The UBCJ president claimed the second proposal would have conceded $1.40 an hour in wages and that the total package would have saved RCA $1 million. After the company rejected the offer and publicly announced the closing, the president said to the *Herald Journal*:

> My feeling is that no matter what we offered the company it would have been rejected. I feel RCA had already decided to close the plant when they told us to start negotiating. Union officials were just strung along from the beginning. RCA would not even tell us what they wanted in the way of concessions (McDonough, July 23, 1982).

On July 22, 1982, RCA announced that its plant in Monticello would close on October 15, 1982. In addition, 28 RCA workers were immediately laid-off in conformance with earlier decisions. In a press release, RCA officials announced the plant would close because ". . . of changing product demands, high manufacturing costs and continuing major capital requirements." The Division Vice President of Manufacturing for the RCA Consumer Electronics Division said that company and union representatives had been meeting to consider workers' recommendations to keep the plant open. He said that at least five factors affected the final decision to close:

1. The age of the plant which was originally built in 1910.
2. Consumer cabinet demand had changed from large console television sets to smaller units.
3. Imports from the Far East had increased competitive pressures on RCA and most foreign producers have domestic assembly plants allowing them to expand into console models.
4. Higher manufacturing costs have decreased the competitiveness of the Monticello plant. Employee costs continue to represent a higher percentage of the total costs involved in producing a cabinet at the plant.
5. The general trend in television production is toward nonconsole receivers. In 1965, 37% of all color sets used furniture cabinets; in 1981 only 21% used such cabinets (*RCA News*, July 22, 1982).

The Monticello mayor indicated that she had been attempting to forestall the closing as had the Lt. Governor of Indiana. She said the city had offered to assist RCA with its utilities and taxes. Other local businesses including Northern Indiana Public Service Company offered to help as well. She added: "Company officials indicated RCA would not be abruptly leaving the community. Not only did they say they had a commitment to the employees but had a commitment to the community in the way of community programs, activities and charities" (McDonough, July 23, 1982b).

On July 25, 1982, the Executive Director of the Indiana Region IV Development Commission wrote to the Mayor to suggest ways to counter the economic effects of the RCA closing. He suggested the formation of an Economic Development Task Force (consisting of the Mayor, county commissioners, city economic development commission members, Chamber of Commerce representatives, and others). He added that Monticello should place ads in trade journals and newspapers such as the *Wall Street Journal* advertising the availability of the plant and that Monticello should reopen the Comprehensive Employment and Training Act (CETA) program for training unemployed workers and contact vocational schools about worker retraining. Also, the new task force should contact firms that might want to lease or purchase the empty plant.

Shortly after the Mayor received the suggestions, she called a meeting of County Commissioners, City Council members, city Economic Development Commission members, members of the Industrial Development Committee of the Chamber of Commerce as well as the Chamber president, the Area Plan Commissioners, and an Indiana Department of Commerce official. The purpose of the meeting was to establish an Economic Development Task Force. On August 16, the city council empowered the Mayor and other city officials to apply for Community Development Block Grant funds to purchase and run the plant to save jobs in the community.

On August 19, the union president announced that RCA had placed its plant closing decision "in abeyance indefinitely" (McDonough, August 20, 1982c). He noted that union/company negotiations would resume in mid-September on the future of the plant. He speculated that increased production and quality improvements led to the company's reconsideration. "The people care about their work and their product. They have been running a full schedule of good cabinets every day" (Bryant, August 20, 1982a). However, a September 3 story in the *Herald Journal* written by the city editor reported that the Lt. Governor told a press conference in Monticello that the plant would eventually be closed despite upcoming negotiations. The Lt. Governor, claiming to have met with RCA officials, said: "In no case did I get any indication that RCA intends in the long run to continue to operate the Monticello plant or have any needs for its products." He advised the business community in Monticello to plan as if the plant were still closing by seeking to advertise the plant and its skilled work force with prospective buyers.

On September 9, the Mayor wrote the Vice President of Industrial Relations at RCA urging the company to indefinitely postpone the July decision to close its Monticello plant. "I wish to reaffirm the city's offer to RCA to be of whatever assistance we can to you. As I have said before, a decision by RCA to discontinue operation here would be economically devastating to our entire area. Therefore, the city of Monticello's position continues to be that we stand readily available to offer whatever support—including monetary—your company might need" (letter dated September 9, 1982).

Talks between the union and RCA concerning the plants future reopened on September 13. After 11 days of intense bargaining, RCA reinstated its original decision to close its Monticello plant. A two-sentence news release was issued to the press on September 24 stating:

Representatives of RCA and local union #3154 of United Brotherhood of Carpenters and Joiners of America concluded their negotiations today concerning the closing of the Monticello Manufacturing Plant to be effective December 1, 1982. The parties also bargained concerning the effects of the closing on wages, hours, and working conditions of the affected employees.

The public relations director for RCA's Consumer Electronics Division, said of the company/union interactions in September that ". . . the renewed negotiations resulted in the decision to close the plant December 1. Wages, hours, and working conditions were the key components of the negotiations" (*Gerard*, September 30, 1982).

Details of the final RCA closing agreement negotiated by the union were announced on October 3 to a gathering of about 350 workers at a local public school. The union leadership confirmed the December 1 closing date for the plant. According to the union president the closing agreement essentially extended the terms of the ongoing contract until December, 1984. Insurance (life, hospital, surgical, and dental) would be free for 6 months beyond the plant closing and available for a small premium for the next 1½ years. Workers also were to receive severance payments based on pay grade and years of service. Retirement benefits remained as they were.

The president of the union said that workers applauded when they heard the closing terms. He claimed that many plant closings provided for less for its workers than the RCA plant. The agreement "just shows that RCA isn't just dumping the people. It shows the kind of character they have and that they are providing for the people. Of course, we don't agree with the plant closing, but now we understand where they're (company officials) coming from, where before we didn't . . . We understand they closed the factory because of bad sales and the upkeep of the building" (Fisher, October 4, 1982).

RCA had rejected the United Brotherhood of Carpenters and Joiners extensive concessions package in the September negotiations. The package included a 36% wage reduction and end of the dental plan. The company rebutted that even with the givebacks RCA would lose an estimated $1.03 per television console made at the plant in 1983, $4.75 per unit loss in 1984, and $6.81 loss per unit in 1985. The company also claimed it would incur major building maintenance costs in order to remain open.

As to the efforts by the Monticello City Council and the Economic Development Task Force, it was reported in the *Lafayette Journal and Courier* that "The Mayor worked with RCA officials, state and city commerce officials, and local investors to draft a package but, she said, negotiations were cut short in September when RCA announced it might keep RCA open" (Bryant, October 3, 1982b).

On October 4, 1982, 420 RCA workers cast ballots concerning the closing contract: 410 voted in favor of the plan, 4 voted no, and 6 abstained.

The last television cabinet was assembled on November 19 and workers were gradually laid-off as the factory began to close its various departments. As the Union president recalled,

> The Wednesday before Thanksgiving was the last day for those few that were left working at the plant. It was very sad that last week, RCA kept a number of people on so they could receive pay through Thanksgiving. As the departments closed down, people ran out of things to do. Many people were crying as they left the plant for the last time (McDonough, December 1, 1982e).

Monticello at Closing Time

When the RCA television cabinet-making factory closed its doors, a reporter on the local newspaper noted that the closing ". . . will have a profound economic impact on White County." As noted in Chapter 2, RCA had been Monticello's largest and White County's second largest employer. In addition, the White County Treasurer reported that RCA's 1981 payroll of $12.4 million yielded $124,000 through the county's 1% option income tax. RCA also paid $40,000 annually in personal property taxes on their factory equipment. "The real estate tax will remain the same but the personal property tax could be less as equipment is moved out of the building. It shouldn't affect the 1983 tax payments but the county will be hit hard in 1984." He also added that, ". . . White County will really be affected when RCA workers' unemployment benefits run out and they start applying for public assistance. In about six months it will probably be staggering" (McDonough, December 1, 1982e).

As to other possible impacts on the county, the White County Welfare Director predicted, "We are going to see some real bad times. The closing of RCA is a disaster that will be fought in private homes and is going to cause a lot of pain." She said food stamp recipients already had risen between 1981 and 1982; claims for aid to dependent children had increased; suicides and child abuse could increase as well (McDonough, December 1, 1982e).

RCA contributions to White County charities would be lost as well. RCA officials noted that it contributed $10,000 a year to local charities. The United Fund (similar to United Way in other communities) received a contribution from RCA of $6,000; $11,000 was received through employee contributions. In 1982, RCA contributed $7,500 to the United Fund (McDonough, December 1, 1982e).

Views from Social Agencies

The RCA plant closing impacted on social agencies and church-related welfare organizations as they sought to respond to the needs of workers. Those needing services would include displaced RCA workers and those who lost jobs due to declining business in the community. White County services were never as extensive as those in many other Indiana counties so the strain on ongoing programs would be substantial. The Director of Welfare for White County indicated that there was a large increase in food stamps during the first half of 1983. In 1982, approximately $24,000 in stamps were issued monthly and, by the first part of 1983, the monthly average was about $43,000. In June, 1983 the figure had declined to $34,000. She speculated that the summer tourist trade had probably somewhat reduced the level of unemployment. Also she believed that some RCA workers had begun to leave the area and further:

> Unemployment has run out. We've had people move out of their homes or whatever, move in with families, so I think that's part of the reason. We had somewhat of an increase in AFDC but then that's back to roughly what it was about a year ago now. I think it got up to almost 90 and we had been running around 70 or 73, 74.

While the data provided by the White County and State Departments of Welfare do not indicate that 90 households were receiving Aid To Families With Dependent Children (AFDC), Table 3.1 shows a slight increase of the rolls in 1983 over 1982 (in Indiana, AFDC is given only to single parents with children which limits the applicability to RCA workers). Quarterly data showed that 65 households were on AFDC in September, 1982 and 74 by December, 1982 (Indiana's Public Welfare Programs for Fiscal Year, 1983). More substantial increases (and increases more likely to reflect RCA workers) were noted in the number of child welfare cases and households using food stamps in 1983 over 1982. However, a comparative analysis of data for neighboring Jasper County in Table 3.1 indicated that percentage increases in AFDC and Food Stamps were greater in neighboring Jasper County than White County between 1982 and 1983, suggesting that general economic dy-

Table 3.1. AFDC, Food Stamp Caseloads, and Child Welfare in White and Jasper Counties (Households)

Date	AFDC				Food Stamps				Child Welfare			
	White	Percentage Change	Jasper	Percentage Change	White	Percentage Change	Jasper	Percentage Change	White	Percentage Change	Jasper	Percentage Change
June, 1980	60	—	66	—	167	—	345	—	NA	—	32	—
June, 1981	65	8	102	54	197	18	372	8	45	—	32	0
June, 1982	71	9	86	-16	240	22	385	3	33	-27	29	-9
June, 1983	73	3	109	27	271	13	475	23	44	33	31	7
June, 1984	72	-1	109	—	256	-6	503	6	32	-27	35	13

Source: White County Welfare Department, *Indiana's Public Welfare Programs for Fiscal Years, 1984, 1983, 1982, 1981, 1980.*

Table 3.2. Food Stamp Program: Total Stamps Issued

County	Fiscal Year ($)		Percentage
	1982	1983	
White	266,280	411,342	54.5
Jasper	591,713	785,264	32.7

Source: Indiana's Public Welfare Programs For Fiscal Years 1983, D-4, D-5.

namics in North Central Indiana rather than the RCA closing may explain increases in AFDC, child welfare, and food stamp increases.

Other results were mixed as well. Table 3.2 shows a 54% increase in the dollar value of food stamps issued in White County. While neighboring Jasper County also showed an increase in food stamps issued, the percentage increase was considerably less than White County. Table 3.3 shows the number of individual recipients of food stamps in White and Jasper counties in 1982 and 1983. Again both counties evidenced increases. In this case, the percentage increase in persons receiving food stamps was greater in Jasper (28%) than White County (19%).

While some of the aggregate data does not suggest particular plant closing impacts on White County, various representatives of county and city social agencies argued that community and workers were seriously affected by the closing. Interviews with representatives of various agencies provided information on anecdotal impacts of the closing not discernible in aggregate data *and* indications of perceived impacts, sometimes not confirmed by the data. The executive director of the White County United Fund pointed to a declining tax base, both prop-

Table 3.3. Individuals Receiving Food Stamps

County	Date	General Public Recipients	AFDC Recipients	Total Recipients	Percentage Change in Total Recipients
White	June, 1983	722	64	786	19
	June, 1982	562	101	663	—
Jasper	June, 1983	1,399	212	1,611	28
	June, 1982	1,063	196	1,259	—

Source: Indiana's Public Welfare Program For Fiscal Year 1982, 1983.

erty and income, and increased demands for public services at a time when United Fund resources would decline. She also predicted that telephone calls to an emergency service, Contact Help, would increase. She reported increased requests for food stamps, and the county had opened a food pantry in June, 1983 where local people could receive food and other assistance. In 2 months they had served 63 families. As to the United Fund itself, the Executive Director had indicated that October, 1982 collections totaled $67,000, an $8,000 decline from 1981.

The United Fund Executive Director also spoke of the crisis in people's lives caused by the closing. "These are people who have high school kids and mortgages, who simply cannot pick up and leave and go to the great Southwest or Florida or California or wherever the great exodus is heading these days. It's difficult for them because they have so many emotional ties to the community to think about leaving." Some workers had opened their own businesses, while others retired early. The hardest hit, she said, were the cases where both husbands and wives worked at RCA. As to the town as a whole:

> It's not quite so much a company town as perhaps some communities in the Northeast and Southeast have been and are now, but as the largest employer in town RCA was depended upon or expected to be supportive of Little League teams and bowling teams and United Fund and every high school yearbook had an ad in it from RCA and all those little things that don't really show until after they aren't there any more.

She said that other companies had begun to pick up the slack but the impacts on those displaced workers remained:

> And it's sad to see your neighbors leave because they can't afford to stay here any longer and it's sad to see. I guess the worst part of it is to see people who have worked there for 50 years who spent 50—not 50 I'll say 30 years—polishing cabinet tops to know that there's no place for them in this society now, in any kind of industry.

One minister involved in emergency assistance programs and a telephone crisis center in White County indicated in July, 1983 that requests for emergency food and shelter increased because RCA worker unemployment benefits had begun to run out. There was more need for help with rent, utilities, and food. The minister claimed that social service agencies, including the United Fund, were receiving some increased contributions from local businesses to compensate for the loss of RCA funds and declining federal support for social programs. As to the crisis center, the Minister indicated that calls in April through June 1983 had increased about 50 per month. Information provided by the telephone crisis center indicated that calls categorized as involving "mental and emotional health" and "basic life necessities" increased in April through June 1983 over earlier months in 1983. However, comparing total calls between January to June 1982 with total calls from January to June 1983, indicated the former period had 25 more calls (766 to 741) than the latter period, which was after the plant closing (Twin Lakes Contact-Help).

Another minister indicated that the White County Food Pantry was formed 1 year before the RCA plant closing. The Food Pantry was created to allow the community at large to participate in purchasing and distributing food to the needy. With the RCA closing, the Minister approached the Ministerial Association to expand the Food Pantry. The newly expanded pantry opened in June 1983. About 20 churches joined, providing money, food, and volunteers, with referrals coming from area pastors. The Food Pantry worked with the Council on Aging and the Christian Assistance Fund to secure a $13,000 emergency food and shelter grant. The Food Pantry received $5,000 of the grant which it used to purchase food supplies.

The Minister reported that requests for food aid from the Food Pantry and mortgage aid from the Christian Assistance Fund had increased as a result of the RCA closing. ". . . In the last two weeks I've had four or five people come to me who had worked at RCA, their unemployment ran out the next week. They had no income whatsoever and they would be eligible for food stamps from Welfare but some of them are almost too proud to have to go ask for help, but they had no choice, especially where there are children involved. And so the Food Pantry has been very busy to help out."

The Director of the Youth Services Bureau claimed that United Fund lost a considerable amount of money due to the RCA closing. RCA was the first or second largest donor in the county. The Youth Services Bureau received a cut of $6,000 in 1982 because United Fund did not achieve its fund-raising goals. Youth Services then was forced to end employee insurance, eliminate a paid secretary, as well as institute other organizational changes.

In addition, the Director stressed the impacts of the closing on the physical and mental health of the unemployed who utilize Youth Service Bureau resources. When former RCA-employed parents attended support group meetings or when they came to the Bureau with their children ". . . not only are they depressed about not having a job but just saying well, there's nothing available, there's nothing to do. Then on top of it, they experience problems within the family. I think it's not the cause of it but it adds to the pressure of dealing with their teenagers or younger children because the financial burden has created stress for everybody. The child can no longer do those things that he's been used to doing—belonging to clubs, belong to this, and that and everything." She argued that younger workers with families may have been more affected by the closing than older workers with seniority ". . . because they've not had the extended unemployment benefits that a lot of the older people manage to get with their seniority and of course they (the older workers) weren't laid off until the last."

The general perspective from the social agencies concerning the impacts of the RCA closing on the community at large and the workers is mixed. Some aggregate data concerning AFDC showed limited change after the closing; other data such as that concerning food stamp use was more dramatic.

Tables 3.4, 3.5, and 3.6 indicate no clear pattern concerning changed levels of auto accidents, death rates, and child abuse cases. Auto accidents in White County declined in 1983 contrary to expectations that accidents would increase after the December, 1982 closing. However, 1984 and 1985 accident levels increased substantially. The possible linkages between delayed effects of the closing including stress and accidents cannot be discerned from the data. The data on death rates are inconclusive as well. Monticello death rates from all causes declined from 1981 through 1985. Death rates from heart and liver ailments declined in 1983 from 1982 while deaths from heart ailments increased in 1984 and declined from liver ailments. Cancer deaths rose in 1983 and declined in 1984. Because of the ambiguous trends in White County and Monticello limiting the possibility of drawing any inferences about

Table 3.4. Auto Accidents, White County

Year	Total Accidents	Fatal Accidents	Total Killed	Personal Injury Accidents
1980	627	7	12	186
1981	676	8	9	175
1982	718	9	11	152
1983	687	5	5	145
1984	777	9	10	180
1985	839	5	6	204

Source: Indiana State Police.

Table 3.5. Death Rates for Selected Causes (White County and Monticello)

Year	Specific Causes (per 100,000)					
	All Causes (per 1,000)	Heart	Cancer	Accident's (not motor)	Suicide	Cirrhosis of Liver
White County						
1980	10.6	439.3	196.7	20.3	4.2	4.2
1981	10.8	390.8	243.7	25.2	8.4	8.4
1982	10.4	428.6	205.9	8.4	12.6	12.6
1983	10.3	393.3	188.3	20.9	12.6	12.6
1984	10.4	392.4	177.2	33.8	8.4	4.2
1985	10.6	395.7	221.3	29.8	17.0	12.8
Monticello						
1980	15.0	538.5	269.2	57.7	0	0
1981	17.5	576.9	403.8	19.2	19.2	19.2
1982	16.5	711.5	288.5	0	0	38.5
1983	15.8	566.0	320.8	37.7	18.9	18.9
1984	14.4	634.6	153.8	38.5	0	0
1985	14.2	615.4	269.2	57.7	38.5	19.2

Source: Indiana Public Health Service.

Table 3.6. Substantiated Child Abuse and Neglect Cases: White and Jasper Counties

	Abuse Cases		Neglect Cases	
	White	Jasper	White	Jasper
1982	6	4	7	9
1983	10	12	9	11
1984	12	9	28	25

Source: Tippecanoe County: Department of Public Welfare.

the relationship between the closing and accidents and deaths, no data for neighboring Jasper County was gathered on these measures.

Table 3.6 shows that child abuse cases did rise in 1983 and 1984 in White County and fell in Jasper County in 1984. Trends in child neglect cases rose in a parallel fashion in the two counties between 1982 and 1984.

Also concerning other data for which there was a comparative standard, such as in food stamps, the directions and magnitudes of changes were as notable for neighboring Jasper County as for White County. The comparison data suggests that plant closing impacts in White County may parallel the impacts of economic recession elsewhere such that the general economy, not any particular economic event, triggered increased demands on social services and crises in people's lives. Consequently, the data may provide support for the research of Brenner (1973) who analyzes aggregate data to discern relationships between changes in unemployment rates and changes in death rates, antisocial behavior, etc. The national and/or state trends may have had a greater impact on Monticello and White County than the RCA closing alone.

On the other hand, most of the social service representatives interviewed (as well as workers and business people) in White County emphasized the deleterious effects of the RCA closing on White County and Monticello. Given the proximity of these persons to the situation, it suggests that aggregate data may not adequately reflect community and individual suffering.

Impacts on the Business Community

Business people have a unique perspective to bring to bear on a community. They see the closing from the vantage point of the local economy and the effects on consumers. Generally those interviewed saw the economic impacts to the community as negative but saw the community recovering from the loss in the future.

One business executive with a public utility company pointed out at the time of the interview (7 months after the closing) that severance pay and unemployment insurance had muted the economic impacts of the closing on the workers and the business community. He suggested that ". . . anytime you layoff that many people why naturally it's going to have a real impact." A banker indicated that the scope of the impact would not be clearly manifested until unemployment benefits ran out. As of June 22, 1983, he claimed, no mortgages had been foreclosed. The low number of foreclosures could also have related to the fact that many of the older workers owned their own homes.

A public utility executive indicated that given the frozen tax rates in Indiana, there would be a shortfall in local revenues. As to the United Fund, it was speculated that contributions would be declining. United Fund contributions in 1982 were already significantly less than 1981. "They've appealed to other industry, other business, individual citizens of the community to try to increase their contribution, to try to offset some of that. And some of that's been done I think, but not to a degree of compensating for what they would have received from RCA." This respondent also reported that delinquency on utility accounts with the public service company had increased but not in the same proportions as the unemployment rate. He further argued that town business had suffered throughout the 1980–1982 recession and that prospects for local recovery were good.

> I think business is down, but I think it has been for a year and a half or two years which goes back prior to when the RCA plant closed. We're constantly looking for new business to come in. We have a few holes down town that are not filled but that we try to keep those occupied if we possibly can and I think that if you look at Monticello and the number of vacant buildings—business buildings downtown—we're in fairly good shape compared to many communities that I'm familiar with.

An executive officer of another industrial plant who was interviewed in July, 1983 said that there are many people in Monticello who still could not believe that RCA and the 800 jobs were gone forever. He speculated that

> . . . the people that were affected the most I would have to guess are the small retail people in terms of merchandising and service such as your plumbers and hardware people, electricians, and motor rewinders and what have you. All those people have to be hurt somehow because we as industry rely upon the local small people for those things an awful lot for the nuts and bolts that we don't have that we should have and repair items.

He said that job loss and movement from the community may harm supermarkets and clothing stores as well but there was no indication of an impact of the closing as of the date he was interviewed. He expressed hope that with an economic upturn, the jobs lost from the RCA closing would be absorbed. Similarly he felt that losses of RCA contributions to the United Fund could be absorbed.

The publisher of the local newspaper indicated that a few stores had closed since RCA left Monticello and the plant closing emotionally affected shoppers and store owners. He said that newspaper circulation had not declined since December, 1982. Generally, however, he believed that any short-term business declines would be overcome. "I hear comments about things will be tough and that was last December when they closed—in '82. We're making an effort, some of us who own properties downtown to bring the stores back to life under new ownership/management." He expressed a general optimism about the future of Monticello's economy:

> We'll bounce back, I'm confident. We will bounce back. We've always been healthy. I grew up here in the depression, I'm a five generation kid. We didn't realize we had a depression when I was a boy. RCA was then owned by a D.D. Ryder, he was a great salesman. He had up to 600 employees back in 31, 33, 34, 35 along in there. He hired them from Southern Indiana. They were wood workers in Southern Indiana, so we have three generations of wood workers here now. A lot of them without work.

Another perspective on the impacts of the plant closing on the business community was discerned when 38 town business people were interviewed about the effects of the RCA closings on their businesses and that of their colleagues. Overwhelmingly (34) the respondents said the closing had at least some impact on business. Their collective estimate was that clothing stores would be most affected with food stores affected least. Thirty business people indicated that RCA workers were customers with about 35% of the respondents indicating that at least moderate amounts of business was accounted for by the RCA workers before the closing. Of the respondents, 63% said that their total sales were affected by the plant closing with 26% stating that the effects were significant. Finally, 47% of the respondents said that citizens of Monticello were spending less because of their fears about the economy.

Table 3.7 shows empirically the sales levels in retail stores of White and Jasper Counties for 1980 to 1983. Total retail sales increased by 3.8% in 1983 over 1982 in White County and less than 1% in neighboring Jasper County. Given 1982–1983 inflation rates, sales in White County evidenced no increase. Sales actually declined in 1983 in eating and drinking establishments, general merchandise, and drugs. In Jasper County, sales declined in 1983 for food, eating and drinking, and general merchandise. Consequently, retail sales did not show significant growth in either county, which suggests that the general recession may have had a stronger effect on these two counties than the plant closing did on White County. The RCA plant closing may have affected business in White County but so did the general level of unemployment and economic recession.

Table 3.7. Retail Sales in White and Jasper Counties 1980–1983

	Total Retail Sales ($)	Food ($)	Eating & Drinking ($)	General Merchandise ($)	Furniture and Appliances ($)	Automotive ($)	Drugs ($)
White County							
1983	97,548	26,343	10,911	8,688	2,505	14,210	4,668
1982	94,003	25,341	11,421	8,779	2,366	11,514	4,940
1981	86,212	20,596	9,282	8,403	2,546	11,578	4,256
1980	74,951	17,500	8,288	7,247	2,236	10,297	3,765
Jasper County							
1983	135,522	29,117	10,918	6,952	1,488	15,156	6,834
1982	134,868	29,192	11,419	7,184	1,465	14,514	6,552
1981	120,970	23,810	10,361	5,805	1,510	13,185	5,517
1980	111,713	21,425	9,297	5,301	1,405	12,417	5,169

Source: Survey of Buying Power, 1984, 1983, 1982, 1981, Sales and Marketing Management.

The Workers Respond

Those most immediately hurt by the plant closing, of course, were the RCA work force itself. A Workers Aid Council (WAC) was created and expanded its activities to meet their needs. The WAC came about after the completion of closing arrangements with RCA as members of the UBCJ Local 3154 began to consider providing support for members who would shortly be facing economic and psychological problems. A labor representative to the United Way in Lafayette, Indiana, had suggested the establishment of a support group within the union to aid those having problems. As a result of the idea, UBCJ Local 3154 established the WAC with an office in the Union Hall in October, 1982. Ten union activists volunteered to serve on the Council. They received 40 hours of evening training for a period of weeks on available state, local, and community services so they could pass information on to members of the local.

One of the WAC members described the broad range of services the Council provided:

> We directed (them) toward food stamps, legal services out of Lafayette. We could also tell them whether they were or weren't (eligible). We could tell if they were making too much money to even bother the welfare office. You know, you could figure it out on paper once they showed us how. We also tried to help them in money management, how to cut down on their groceries, how to buy the cheapest grades of stuff and how to cook it, prepare it. How to budget your money, talk to the bill collectors, how to stretch your money, and get them to take half payments or interest only payments and things like this that if you go talk to them they'll usually meet you more than half way.

This WAC member indicated that soon after the plant closing she was receiving 10 to 20 calls a week. After a time the frequency of calls slackened but accelerated dramatically at about the time that unemployment benefits began to run out. WAC services were provided not only to RCA workers but also to any needy person in the county.

> I had a lot of people here in Monon that I don't even know who they were. They would come in and talk to me and I could tell them: Yes you can go over here or yes you can go over there. Or your income's too high. That can't help. But call Legal Services or something like that. And I don't even know who they were.

This member indicated that she talked to two people who even mentioned suicide as a solution to their problems.

Along with counseling workers, filling out forms for welfare and food stamps, and taking people to the county welfare office, WAC members just listened to problems that were experienced by all the workers. According to a council member: "And then I think a lot of people got a lot of benefit from just being able to talk to other people that were in the same boat. It always helped to say it out loud, I think." Another member pointed out that workers could more easily talk to one of their fellow workers than some stranger in a government office. Consequently, WAC would often aid and serve as a "liaison" for the individual worker in his or her dealings with a governmental agency. For example, the WAC arranged with the Indiana Employment Security Division in Logansport, Indiana to send an officer to Monticello once a week to process White County unemployment claims. This regular appearance of the unemployment officer saved workers time and gasoline costs.

One of the most active WAC members, a former shop steward at RCA, indicated that the union leadership was interested in getting "troublemakers" on the WAC. The idea was to select a committee that ". . . wouldn't stand for any pushing around or be pushed . . ." particularly in dealing with government agencies or the company. This member also indicated his own strong commitment to help others and "to get involved with their personal lives." He said that, "That's what we was there for—to help people and we done what we set out to do." Another member indicated that she was chosen for the WAC because "they know I was outspoken and the union knew I was outspoken and that's the type of people they wanted." WAC members, she said, were chosen with an eye toward problems with agencies, such as the Welfare Department, with whom confrontation would be needed on occasion.

The most involved WAC members said they wanted to help others, to acquire information that they could personally use, and to keep busy. One member summarized the many benefits of the WAC:

> No, it didn't make it difficult. It helped the family because I wasn't working. When I'm not working you know you get bored looking at four walls and you get grumpy. So it's a chance to get away from the kids and away from home and still learn and be able to help other people. And if I got into any situation then I would know how to handle it myself. So it really helped more than anything.

Along with counseling individuals, the WAC confronted recalcitrant officials in agencies such as welfare and unemployment and shared their experiences with other union locals in White and Tippecanoe Counties. Occasionally, the WAC engaged in attempts to pressure business people and governmental officials to aid the displaced workers. For example, the WAC organized a meeting of community leaders and politicians on April 25, 1983. They met prior to the arrival of the guests at the Union Hall to plan strategy. Different WAC members (only five WAC members came early) were assigned to ask questions of the banker, the mayor, the state legislators, a congressman, and a representative of one of Indiana's senators. Also in May, 1983, the WAC organized a panel discussion on vocational training opportunities for displaced workers. Finally, WAC members participated in the securing of a government-sponsored job search training program, Project Care, to be administered at the Union Hall.

As Project Care (Community Action for Retraining and Employment) developed, the activities of the WAC tended to be less distinctive and visible. Project Care occupied most of the space in the Union Hall and the WAC activities receded to the background. However, White County workers continued to communicate with the more active WAC members if they had problems. One member reported that he was still getting at least one call a week nearly a year after the shutdown. Another member indicated that many workers knew that WAC activists were good resource people and hence continued to rely on their help. Consequently, while the WAC dissolved by the fall of 1983, the three or four most active members continued to provide needed services to displaced workers.

Project Care

During the spring of 1983, members of the Northwest Central Labor Council (NWCLC) and the newly established Displaced Workers Assistance Agency (DWAA), in Lafayette, Indiana, and researchers at Purdue University learned of possible funding through the Comprehensive Education and Training Act (CETA) for job search training programs. The closing of three Kroger grocery stores in the Lafayette area in February, 1983 led to the visit, in Lafayette, by a staff person from the United Food and Commercial Workers (UFCW). While his first concern was helping displaced Kroger workers, the UFCW representative participated in discussions concerning a job search program for both La-

fayette and Monticello. Labor and university people then came together to write the proposal calling for a Project Care (Community Action
for Retraining and Employment). The original proposal was to provide
job search skills for the former Kroger and RCA workers. The admin-
istering and funding agency funded the proposal for training only
Monticello RCA workers. Consequently, Project Care was targeted pri-
marily for those 828 RCA workers who lost their jobs because of the
plant closing (and 23 other unemployed workers in the Monticello area
who were eligible for the program). The time frame of the Project Care
program was June 1, 1983 through September 30, 1983 with a total cost
of $73,716.00.

Project Care identified six elements of the 4-month program: (1) con-
tacting all displaced RCA workers; (2) assessing the employment and
training needs of the displaced workers; (3) building links with retraining institutions like Purdue University and the nearby vocational college; (4) referral of workers to appropriate courses; (5) enrolling participants in job clubs to aid placement, and (6) providing follow-up support
and services to program participants. The program was conducted at
the UBCJ Local 3154 Union Hall and nearby public school building. A
member of the Displaced Workers Assistance Agency (created by the
Northwest Central Labor Council) was chosen to be a salaried project
director. He selected a professional person to help administer the program. Four other paid staff people included the president of Local 3154,
one member of the WAC, a third member of Local 3154, and a displaced Kroger worker from UFCW Local 25 in Lafayette.

Of the 828 laid-off RCA workers and the other eligible workers in
the community, 227 participated in some phase of the job training. The
six phases of the program included an orientation, intake, assessment,
two workshops, and the Job Club. One hundred and six displaced
workers participated in all six phases. Among the 227 people who attended at least one stage in the program, 73 found jobs. Of these, 62%
or 45 workers participated in all program phases including the Job Clubs.

The most significant phase of Project Care was the Job Clubs, which
were groups of workers, not exceeding 12, who met for two or three
half days a week. In the Job Clubs, job seekers made simulated calls to
possible employers and received collective criticism. After compiling
lists of possible places to work, they then called prospective employers
while others observed them.

Of the 73 displaced workers who found new jobs, the most typical
work included the following: truck driver, warehouse attendant, jani-
tor, cook, cashier, dishwasher, factory assembler, mechanic's assistant,
commission-earning sales person, teacher's aid, and self-employed

businessman. The most striking data about this reemployment was that of the 67 former RCA workers who found work after Project Care, 55% of them were earning less than $5 an hour. Prior to the layoffs these RCA workers were earning about $8 an hour.

While Project Care did not provide high-paying jobs, or indeed any jobs for the majority of the displaced RCA work force, it was responsible for a number of accomplishments. First, labor and allies of labor were instrumental in obtaining the grant to run the program. Second, three union members participated in program administration. Third, some participants actually got jobs as a result of the program. Fourth, over 200 displaced workers learned some skills related to job searching. Finally, Project Care illustrated the continuing attempts of the union local to provide support to its members in the face of adversity, much as the Workers Aid Council had.

Conclusion

The RCA plant closed on December 1, 1982 ending employment for some 800 workers. Government officials noted impacts on taxes; social agency personnel warned of declining support for the United Fund and other local organizations. Workers organized quickly to serve their co-workers; friends of labor and organized labor established Project Care. As to impacts on workers, business, and the community at large, some respondents were pessimistic about the future as unemployment benefits and severance pay ran out. A few were optimistic about the long-term capacity of the Monticello economy to recover. As to AFDC, child welfare, and food stamps, short-term changes were noted in the aftermath of the closing. Concerning auto accidents, health, and psychological problems no discernible impacts on Monticello were noted based upon aggregate data. Of those indicators where comparisons with neighboring Jasper County were made, trends differed little. The aggregate data suggested that negative economic change in White County probably resulted from the general recession in Indiana and the nation as well as the RCA plant closing. The anecdotal evidence reflected in the perceptions of social agency personnel, religious leaders, business people, and workers indicated the specific suffering to workers and the community caused by the closing.

4

ECONOMIC EFFECTS ON WORKERS

The previous chapter gauged the "ripple" effects of the plant closing on the community in which it was located. The present chapter documents the impact of the shutdown on those most immediately affected, namely, the displaced workers and their families. In a closing all workers lose their jobs; however, there is variability among workers in the length of their unemployment and in the nature of their new jobs, if they become reemployed (Aronson and McKersie, 1980; Bluestone and Harrison, 1982; Flaim and Sehgal, 1985; Lipsky, 1979; Nowak and Snyder, 1983). Less is known about other aspects of the economic impact, such as the extent of displaced workers' access to alternative sources of income other than their jobs, their subjective experience of economic distress or their economic coping strategies (Larson, 1984; Pearlin and Schooler, 1978; Rayman, 1982; Rosen, 1983; Weeks and Drengacz, 1982). Moreover, few studies compare economic effects of closings for blue-collar workers by gender (Aronson and McKersie, 1980; Bluestone and Harrison, 1982; Liem and Rayman, 1982; Lipsky, 1979; Rayman, 1982; Nowak and Snyder, 1983) or by age (Aronson and McKersie, 1980; Flaim and Sehgal, 1985; Lipsky, 1979).

Our RCA study examines effects in terms of all the economic factors mentioned above, namely, length of unemployment, reemployment status, income loss, perceived economic distress, cutbacks in consumer expenditures, and increased engagement in money-saving activities. For each we systematically compare the experiences of displaced workers of different age and gender. In addition, for the three latter factors, comparisons between the reemployed and the still unemployed are made. The format of this chapter is to review the relevant literature regarding each economic effect and then to present our own findings.

Length of Unemployment

A recent government survey of 5.1 million workers displaced between 1979–1984 (i.e., workers having at least 3 years on the job before losing it to plant closings or job cutbacks) found that their median length of time without work was 24 weeks. About one-fourth of the workers were without work for 1 year or more during the 5-year period (Office of Technology Assessment, 1986). Moreover, an Indiana study of workers who were displaced by the 1972 closing of Drewrys Brewery of South Bend found that only 55% had found full-time, permanent jobs in the area by 1979 (7 years later) (Craypo and Davisson, 1983).

The few studies which compare economic effects of plant closings for blue-collar women as well as men are somewhat consistent in finding a longer period of unemployment following job loss for women than men (Aronson and McKersie, 1980; Lipsky, 1979; Nowak and Snyder, 1983). It is often suggested that being married gives women economic protection which permits longer job search and, hence, longer duration of unemployment, but the findings are not clear. For example, Lipsky (1979) found longer unemployment for single workers; whereas, Aronson and McKersie (1980) found longer unemployment for those who had another wage earner in the household, most often the spouse. A third study (Rosen, 1983) which focused on *women* only, examined effects of displacement, both permanent and temporary. Among the displaced workers, married women were as likely as the single women to look for work and to become reemployed (60% reemployed between 5–9 months after displacement), and most of these were being recalled to their former companies and jobs.

Length of unemployment is also longer for relatively older workers in comparison to younger ones (Aronson and McKersie, 1980; Flaim and Sehgal, 1985; Lipsky, 1979). The former tend to have less formal education and more on-the-job training skills, which may be less transferable to new job settings. They may also be less able to be retrained and less willing to relocate geographically (Flaim and Sehgal, 1985; Gordus, 1984).

Only 60% of a large, nationwide sample of workers displaced from 1979–1983 were reemployed by January, 1984. Twenty-five percent were

Table 4.1. Reported Sources of Income Nine Months After Shutdown

Source of Income	Percentage	N
Own present job	24.5	80
Spouse's salary	37.6	123
Own unemployment compensation	71.3	233
Spouse's unemployment compensation	18.0	59
Severance pay from RCA	43.4	142
Pensions (including Social Security)	6.7	22
Savings	48.0	157
Rental income	2.8	9
Income from investments	6.1	20
Borrowing on life insurance	4.9	16
Borrowing from family/friends	15.6	51
Borrowing on house mortgage	1.8	6
Food stamps	11.0	36
Public assistance	5.8	19
Child support/alimony	4.9	16
Other	11.9	39

still unemployed and 14% had dropped out of the labor force. In comparison to men, women were less likely to have found new jobs. Younger workers were more likely than older workers to be reemployed (Flaim and Sehgal, 1985, p. 6 and Table 4.1).

In our sample of displaced RCA workers, 71% were still unemployed 8 months after the plant closed; 17% were reemployed full-time, 12% part-time. Among those who were laid off about 1 year before the plant closed, 54% were still unemployed 20 months later; 28% were reemployed on a full-time basis; 18% on a part-time basis. Among those displaced at the time of the closing, 75% were still unemployed 8 months later; 16% were reemployed as full-time workers, 10% as part-time workers.

The female workers, who had fewer years of service with RCA than the men (12 vs. 19 years, on the average), were, in general, laid off prior to the closing. Even though they had had more time in which to search for new jobs, the women were less likely than the men to be reemployed full-time (11 vs. 25%, respectively).

The following example gives one woman's reason for the length of her unemployment.

31-year-old married woman

There are still a lot of us R.C.A. workers unemployed . . . and there are no jobs for us, only jobs at minimum wage and after I pay for a babysitter for three children and gas for the job I have nothing left for bills and food.

Age of workers was also related to date of layoff from RCA and reemployment. The younger workers were laid off earlier and were more likely to be reemployed. Less time to search for a new job, however, was not the only obstacle to reemployment among the older workers. That is, among those displaced last (between 8 and 9 months when contacted), older workers (age 55+) were more likely to still be unemployed (92%) than younger (age 35–44) workers (61%).

The following comments from older workers who were still unemployed reflect an awareness of the difficulty older displaced workers generally face in seeking reemployment.

56-year-old married woman

I feel that I have been affected by the plant closing. I am 56 years old and it's hard to go get another job at that age. I had planned to work another ten years. Can't draw Social Security until you're 62. I will be out of unemployment compensation soon. I am glad we have our home paid for. I would rather be working. I feel we have a good Union. I feel the Government should help get more jobs going.

57-year-old married man

My wife and I were doing very well before RCA laid me off in April 1981. In November, 1981, her plant closed. We had some money saved and have been using it to supplement her part-time work. Employers say they don't discriminate but my age is the biggest factor why I haven't been hired, I believe. I will keep looking and hopefully will find employment.

Thus, consistent with our expectations derived from the literature, a majority of the former RCA workers were still unemployed 8 months subsequent to the plant closing. Moreover, both gender and age of the displaced workers were important influences on subsequent employment status, with women and relatively older workers being less likely than men and youth to have obtained reemployment.

Income Loss

An additional economic cost of shutdowns is lower income for the displaced workers. This results not only from the period of unemployment and reemployment at lower wages and/or reduced hours, but also from longer, more frequent periods of unemployment because of loss of seniority and greater probability of job dissatisfaction (Ashton and Iadicola, 1986). Nationally, among workers displaced from 1979 to 1983 who found new full-time jobs, 45% had taken reductions in pay and, for 30%, these cuts were one-fifth or more of their former earnings. In addition, a substantial number had become reemployed in part-time jobs. Taking both full- and part-time workers into account, at least one-half of the reemployed workers were earning less than before displacement (Flaim and Sehgal, 1985). An Indiana study of reemployed blue-collar workers, who were displaced by the shutdown of the Fort Wayne International Harvester plant, found that 74.6% reported a loss of earnings when comparing income of current job to that of highest paid job at the plant, and 65.4% earned less at the current job compared to the last job at the plant (Ashton and Iadicola, 1986). An earlier Indiana study of blue-collar workers who were displaced by the closing of Drewrys Brewery in South Bend found that of those who were reemployed on a full-time, permanent basis 7 years following the shutdown, 77% reported a loss of wages when comparing income of current job to wages they had earned at the brewery.

Income loss applies to displaced women as well as men, as indicated by Rosen's findings that the average blue-collar female worker laid off from New England clothing and electrical goods industries lost 20% of her annual income in the year following job loss (cited in Office of Technology Assessment, 1986). Moreover, reemployment, when it occurs for women, tends to be more in sales and service jobs, rather than more in production work, as in the case of men (Bluestone and Harrison, 1982; Liem and Rayman, 1982; Nowak and Snyder, 1983). The Rosen (1983) study found, to the contrary, that most displaced women who took new jobs, rather than returning to their former jobs, were hired into production jobs, not in sales and service. These differences probably reflect the context of the unemployment and the local employment opportunities.

In general, younger workers and those with more education were less likely than their counterparts to experience a loss in earnings and total income loss (Ashton and Iadicola, 1986; Flaim and Sehgal, 1985).

Overall, our sample of displaced workers had been earning about

$12,000 in the year prior to the shutdown, while their total family income averaged $20,000. Partly because of having greater service at RCA, men's 1982 income greatly exceeded women's ($15,000 vs. $11,000). However, total family income was similar for displaced men and women ($20,000, on the average). Similarly, older workers earned more than younger ones.

All workers contributed substantially to their family's 1982 income, although male workers contributed a larger proportion than did women (81 vs. 63%). For married workers, the men earned 78% of the family income; the women earned 49%. Similarly, the older the workers, the greater their contribution to the total family income.

Displaced workers reported having a variety of alternative sources of income at the time of our survey (see Table 4.1). The only source available to a majority (71%) was unemployment compensation, paid to those who were still unemployed at the time of our survey. In addition, 43% of the workers reported that they still had not spent all of their severance pay.

Assets in the form of income from rentals and investments, or life insurance or home mortgages against which money could be borrowed were available to a small percentage of the displaced workers. Forty-eight percent had savings on which they could draw. At the other end of the continuum, 11% were depending on food stamps and 5.8% on public assistance as sources of income.

Regarding resources of women in comparison to those of men, it has already been noted that the former were less likely than the latter to have found new jobs. On the other hand, women were more likely to receive child support (8.3 vs. 0.7%) and pensions (10.6 vs. 2.1%).

Some sources of financial support were more likely for older than younger workers, namely, unemployment compensation, unspent severance pay from RCA, and pensions and income from investments. However, a comparable percentage of older and younger workers were receiving food stamps and public assistance. In addition, the age groups were similar in the percentages reporting savings, rental income, and ability to borrow on life insurance and home mortgages. Younger workers were more likely to have a new job, to have an employed spouse, and child support as sources of income. They also were more likely than older workers to feel that they could borrow money from family and friends.

For the minority of displaced workers who were reemployed, either full- or part-time, one estimate of whether or not they have recovered financially could be made by comparing their 1983 with their 1982 weekly salaries. Among those who worked nearly all of 1982, men were earning 67% of their former weekly salaries; women were earning 59%. One women describes her husband's new job in terms of income loss and added expenditures.

48-year-old married woman
My husband because of being laid off had to get a job up North. Therefore, we had to move at a greater expense, with less money. There are no jobs anywhere.

Men's income was higher than women's even when controlling for time these workers have been on their new jobs, an average of 4.3 and 1.7 months, respectively. Regarding age comparisons, younger workers had lost less in terms of new job (1983) wages than had older workers.

One reemployed older worker summarizes his situation in terms of loss of income as well as other benefits.

41-year-old married man
I lost $1.40 an hour. I have to drive to Monon instead of being able to walk if I wanted to. I lost 20 years on a job. It messed my retirement plans up. At the present time I have no health insurance. At my age it's harder to get a good job to support my family proper. I was counting on R.C.A. life insurance.

Another still unemployed older worker predicts he will be working for lower wages.

50-year-old single man
At the present time I feel I'm going to be working for less wages than I have in the past (if working at all). That will make my social security less.

The first statement reveals some of the additional problems of displaced workers who become reemployed. Since this respondent took a new job he lost the health insurance that was provided by the closing contract and was not provided with health insurance by the new employer.

Perceived Economic Distress

In contrast to actual income loss, workers perceive themselves to be experiencing financial hardship to one degree or another. Such psychological perception of being in economic distress, is greater among un-employed workers than employed men and women (Schlozman, 1979). Regarding gender differences, Schlozman found that among the un-employed in general, women were less likely than men (73 vs. 82%) to be dissatisfied with their income. However, among the unemployed who were main wage earners with dependent children, women were *more* likely than men (92 vs. 81%) to be dissatisfied with their income. The other major study of perceived distress is Shamir's (1985) research on married college-educated Israelis. He found that for two subjective evaluations of financial state, the unemployed perceived greater hard-ship than did the reemployed. Moreover, there was a sex-employment status interaction, such that perceptions of financial state were better for unemployed women than for unemployed men.

In our study perceived economic distress is measured by eight cate-gories of consumer items a displaced worker indicated s/he could not afford (for example, the kind of food they/their family should have). Displaced workers noted that they could not afford an average of five of the eight categories listed on our questionnaire. The items that over one-half of the sample were unable to afford were leisure activities (89%); replacement of worn-out furniture or household equipment (78%); clothing (62%); and car (62%). Of the displaced workers, 43% reported that they could not afford the kind of food that they or their families should have.

In contrast, a comparison sample of continuously employed workers at another plant in the community reported they were unable to afford an average of 2.5 of the eight economic categories. For only one cate-gory, leisure activities, did a majority of the comparison sample report having inadequate resources.

The increased economic distress because of unemployment obtained equally for women as well as men. Among the women, the unem-ployed were unable to afford an average of five categories; the contin-uously employed, an average of three. Among the men, the unem-ployed were unable to afford an average of five categories; the continuously employed, an average of two.

Regarding age comparisons, older workers were somewhat less dis-tressed economically than younger ones. In particular, older workers were more likely to report being able to afford a suitable home (and more had a paid up house mortgage) and a car.

Interestingly, currently reemployed workers, both full- and part-time, were somewhat more economically distressed than those still unem-ployed at the time of our study. This may be because their new job income was well below (one-third to one-half) that of their pre-closing RCA wages.

The following comments illustrate the situation of those who can still afford basics but can no longer afford extras.

46-year-old divorced woman

Our home is livable and we get by with groceries, clothing, car, etc. We survive but that is not really living.

42-year-old married woman

The closing at RCA has put a hardship on everyone that worked there. We were able to afford extra items we wanted, but now our pennies have to be watched.

In contrast are the next comments which indicate financial hardship.

54-year-old widowed woman

I have had a hard time paying my bills. I have had my lights and gas turned off because I have not had any money. I hate to beg people to help me because I can not afford to pay my own bills.

53-year-old married man

I just wish we could find a job somewhere so we could keep our rent paid so they won't throw us out in the streets.

Still other comments show concern about economic distress in the future as well as currently.

54-year-old married man

My 26 weeks is about up on my unemployment money. With winter coming on how am I going to keep my utilities paid and bills paid? What is next?

42-year-old married woman

Things weren't too bad last year because of severance pay but I really don't see how we'll make it through this winter. We're a month behind now and I see the hole only getting deeper.

52-year-old married man

So far I have gotten along very well—but we have just about gone through all our savings. If NIPSCO (utility company) doesn't do something about cutting back on their utility bill it will force me to sell my home and move out.

46-year-old divorced woman

How can you explain how you feel when you have only one unemployment check left on your claim? I have a disconnect notice from NIPSCO for $333.95. I went to the Christian Assistance preacher and he said he couldn't help me because I live in Carroll County. What are we supposed to do? Stop existing? I lost my new car after lay-off and the one I have needs to be worked on. I don't know what to do.

Cutbacks in Expenditures

Changes in economic behavior can be viewed as either effects of a shutdown or strategies to cope with changed circumstances. For example, cutbacks in economic expenditures for both essential as well as luxury items were made by 79% of the unemployed in contrast to 51% of the employed in the few months prior to a survey of households in large urban areas (Schlozman and Verba, 1979). A study by Rayman (1982, p. 328) which compared unemployed men and women on expenditures for luxury items only, found men more likely than women to make cutbacks (70 vs. 54%). The author suggested that men could afford more luxuries before job loss and/or were more likely to be the main wage earner. Rosen's (1983, p. 21) study of women only found that job losers cut back more than the employed on nine of twenty-one items and reported cutting back most frequently on groceries and clothing, followed by recreation, vacations, gifts, and household maintenance. Those unemployed women also reported more cutbacks than the employed on insurance and medical care. For older women, the loss of health care benefits and full pensions at retirement was especially difficult. Moreover, Larson's (1984) study of employed and unemployed blue-collar workers and their wives found that the unemployed were more likely to have reduced their expenditures for clothing and education.

In our study the economic effects of unemployment can be reflected in expense adjustments which were made by the displaced individuals and their families (see Table 4.2). For only five of twenty items listed was there stability in expenditures for a majority of the displaced RCA workers; that is, for fire and automobile insurance; children's schooling expenses; child support payments; and rent or house payments.

The more general pattern of economic adjustments among the displaced workers was to cut back or eliminate expenses. The less the workers' (individual or family) income during the year of the shutdown (1982) and the fewer the sources of income they had in the following year (1983), the greater the number of categories of consumer items they felt they could not afford (i.e., the greater their perceived

Table 4.2. Percentage of Displaced Workers Making Expense Adjustments After the Shutdown

	Reduction or Elimination	No Change	Increase in Expenditure
Gifts	92.1	6.5	1.4
Charitable contributions	88.9	9.4	.7
Entertainment	87.4	12.0	.7
Magazines/newspaper	64.0	34.6	1.4
Telephone	48.4	47.0	4.6
Children's schooling	40.5	55.5	4.0
Children's other expenses	67.9	27.0	5.1
Child support/alimony	35.5	62.4	2.2
Clothing	78.1	19.5	2.3
Food	67.1	28.8	4.1
Home maintenance	66.0	28.2	5.8
Rent, house payments	24.9	70.7	4.4
Fire insurance	16.9	78.8	4.2
Own education/training	55.2	36.6	8.3
Auto maintenance	57.7	36.5	5.8
Auto insurance	18.3	77.2	4.5
Dental care	64.5	27.4	8.0
Health care	49.3	43.6	7.1
Health insurance	42.1	41.1	16.8
Life insurance	44.9	45.2	9.9

economic distress). The greater the perceived economic stress, moreover, the more reductions in expenditures which they reported making (data not shown). More specifically, for 11 items, expenditures were reduced or eliminated by more than 50% of the sample—gifts, charitable contributions, entertainment, clothing, children's expenses (other than schooling), food, home maintenance and repair, dental care, magazines or newspapers, auto maintenance and repair, and respondent's education and/or training expenditures. Moreover, 51% wrote in some "other" item for which expenses had been cut and 49% had cut back or eliminated health care.

There was no difference between men and women or the reemployed vs. still unemployed as to the number or kinds of adjustments made. Older age, on the other hand, was related to fewer cutbacks, notably for health insurance and health care. It should be noted that the health insurance which had been provided at the plant was continued by RCA for 1 year for workers as long as they were unemployed and continued to pay for the insurance. Since the older workers were laid off later than younger ones, and were less likely to be reemployed, they were more likely to still have RCA health insurance coverage at the time of our survey.

Currently employed workers were making as many expense adjustments as those who were still unemployed. As was the case for perceived economic distress, continued cutbacks were probably necessitated by the income loss experienced by those who were reemployed.

Home Production

Regarding changes in economic behavior in response to financial difficulties, there is some evidence that temporarily unemployed workers use a variety of strategies to extend household income. For example, Young and Newton (in Weeks and Drengacz, 1982, pp. 310–311) reported that workers laid off from the wood products industry planted vegetable gardens, hunted and fished, and shared household resources, tools, and labor with neighbors. In addition, Larson (1984) found that families of unemployed men compared to families of employed men were more likely to increase the making of clothes at home.

As expected, for our sample of displaced workers there was increased home production; that is, the more workers felt their financial resources were inadequate, the more time they spent on money-saving activities, such as shopping for food bargains and do-it-yourself home repairs. Specifically, the majority of the respondents reported spending more time on seven of nine such activities listed on our questionnaire: shopping for food bargains; shopping for clothing bargains; gardening; preparing meals; canning; home repairs; and car repairs.

The types of activities in which women and men were likely to engage followed a traditional division of labor (Duncan *et al.*, 1973). Specifically, women were more likely than men to shop more for bargains (food and clothing). Women were also more likely than men to be spending more time on preparing meals and canning. In addition, the women were spending more time on sewing. Men were more likely than women to be spending more time on both home and auto repairs.

There were no differences in the home production activities of older and younger workers, or for the reemployed versus the still unemployed.

Summary and Conclusions

At the time of our study, 8 months after the shutdown, a majority of the workers were still unemployed, drawing unemployment compensation as a source of income, and unable to afford numerous consumer items for themselves and/or their families. Their perceived economic stress was accompanied by making reductions in expenditures for both necessary and discretionary goods and services, and by increasing the time spent on money-saving home production activities.

Studies of the economic effects of unemployment from the Great Depression until this decade generally concentrated on the job loss of male breadwinners (Targ, 1983). There continues to be a paucity of studies of unemployed women. Our study contributes to this literature by systematically comparing women with men who have been displaced by a single plant closing in a small, Midwestern town.

Overall, we found that the men and women were affected comparably by job loss following the plant closing. The financial loss was important to workers of each gender because both had contributed substantially to their family's income level before the shutdown. Their perceptions of economic distress and economic coping activities were also comparable.

Like gender, age of workers has received relatively little research attention as an attribute which conditions the impact of displacement. Our study extends knowledge by showing some financial advantages associated with age. That is, because recency of layoff was positively related to age, older workers were more likely than younger ones to still be covered by important company-related benefits, such as severance pay and health insurance. They were also more likely to have a paid-up mortgage on their place of residence, and to feel less economic hardship in general. Such advantages of age, however, may obtain for the short-term only, for with advancing age there is lower likelihood of reemployment and greater likelihood of relative income loss with reemployment, if it occurs.

Finally, in terms of economic impact of the closure, the minority of our respondents who had become reemployed had not nearly recovered their former income levels. Their use of economic coping strategies was as great as for the still unemployed, and their feeling of suffering economic hardship even greater.

It is clear that the workers who were displaced by the closing of the RCA plant were adversely affected economically. The economic hardship was quite important in its own right. It also relates significantly to displaced workers' psychological and physical health problems. Since there is no universal health coverage in the United States, when people such as the former RCA workers lose their jobs, they eventually lose their health benefits, and with lowered income they become unable to afford private medical care. Treatment may be postponed or foregone altogether. In addition, the stresses of job and income loss may attack both mental and physical health, particularly if displaced workers lack social support from family, friends, and community (Perrucci and Perrucci, 1986). It is to the impact of the plant closing on the former RCA workers' health and family relationships to which attention turns in the next chapter.

5

EFFECTS ON WORKERS' HEALTH
AND FAMILY RELATIONSHIPS

In addition to the expected economic hardship caused by plant closings, unemployed workers and their families become vulnerable to
physical health problems, such as stomach trouble or high blood pressure, psychological difficulties, such as depression, and family tension,
which can lead to conflict. The mechanism by which unemployment
causes health problems is not clear. Suggestions have been made that
these problems may be caused either by the economic or by the social
losses which accompany unemployment. One suggestion is that job
loss may result in the loss of income and fringe benefits that had sus-
tained good nutrition and good medical care, thus impacting unfavor-
ably on health (House, 1979). As mentioned in the previous chapter,
research indicates that many of the unemployed make cutbacks in expenditures for food, dental care, medical insurance, and medicine (Rosen, 1983; Rosenblum, 1984; Schlozman, 1979; Schlozman and Verba,
1979). Moreover, Snyder and Nowak (1984) and Rosen (1983) found a
positive relationship between cutbacks and demoralization. The suggestion has also been made that job loss may affect physical and mental health through stress from loss of such things as meaningful work,
self-esteem, social ties, or a routine which structures one's time and
activities (House, 1979; Liem and Liem, 1979). An additional possibility
is that both financial and social factors are related to physical, mental,
and family problems among the unemployed.

In this study we examine a variety of effects on displaced workers'
health and social relationships, including self-reported physical health
problems and psychological problems as indicated by lack of a sense of

mastery over life, loss of social support from family and friends, pessimism about one's economic future, and depression. Effects on marital and familial relationships are also briefly considered. For each factor we compare effects on workers in terms of their gender, age, and current employment status. In addition, we compare the displaced workers to continuously employed workers in a factory in the same town. The chapter format is to review the research literature regarding each effect and then to present our related findings.

Physical Health

Some research regarding the health effects of unemployment concerns plant closings, but more concerns general unemployment. Overall, prior studies of the effect of unemployment on physical health have yielded mixed results. With respect to plant closings, one longitudinal study of two shutdowns examined physical health effects for the displaced blue-collar men (Kasl *et al.*, 1975; Kasl and Cobb, 1979). For a 2-year period, the authors did not find either number of physical symptoms or number of days that a respondent "did not carry on usual activities" due to illness or injury to be related to the length of time since the plant closed. The number of days respondents did not feel well was higher, on the average, for men who subjectively rated the job loss experience as more severe; i.e., said that it took longer "before things got pretty well back to normal" (Kasl *et al.*, 1975, p. 112).

A subsequent analysis of these plant closing data indicated that perceived economic deprivation from unemployment was not correlated with number of symptoms of illness (Gore, 1978).

In contrast, among men and women aircraft industry workers, most of those who had experienced a job loss within 10 years reported "related periods of serious . . . physical strain." Commonly reported forms of physical strain included high blood pressure, alcoholism, increased smoking, and insomnia (Rayman and Bluestone cited in Liem and Rayman, 1982). In addition, at least one-half of the physicians interviewed in south-suburban Chicago, an area of high unemployment, reported finding increased amounts of depression, anxiety, emotional disability, and alcoholism (South Suburban Task Force, 1984). A marked increase in alcohol consumption as indicated by over-the-counter sales of liquor was also reported in relation to a number of closings and layoffs in rural Oregon (Weeks and Drengacz, 1982). An Indiana study of the closing of a South Bend brewery found that one-sixth of the displaced workers (36 of 233) had died during the 7 years subsequent to the shutdown. Some deaths were presumably due to stress associated with the shutdown in that the displaced workers' mortality rate was sixteen times the normal mortality rate for men having the same age distribution (Craypo and Davisson, 1983).

There is some evidence that reemployment, in the short run, positively affects physical health. For four health indicators, such as pulse rate, scores were more negative for men who went from a period of anticipation of a plant closing to unemployment than for men who went from anticipation of a plant closing to immediate reemployment at some other work place. However, there were no traceable long-term effects for these indicators (Kasl and Cobb, 1979).

Regarding age variation in effects, unemployed middle-aged and older workers reported having more days during which they did not feel as well as usual and days during which they did not carry out usual activities due to illness or injury (Kasl *et al.*, 1975).

RCA Findings

We asked the displaced RCA workers if they had experienced any of five specified health-related problems as a result of their layoff. About one-third indicated that they had suffered headaches and one-quarter, gastrointestinal problems. Smaller percentages had experienced high blood pressure and respiratory and heart problems.

Men and women did not differ in the percentage who reported such effects on their health. Age, on the other hand, was related in a curvilinear manner to health problems; that is, the youngest (34 years) and oldest (55 and over) reported suffering somewhat fewer problems than the middle-aged groups of displaced workers (35–44 and 45–54). Specifically, they were less likely to report headaches or stomach problems as a result of job loss. Those who were reemployed at the time of our study reported having had as many ailments as those who were still unemployed.

In addition, 37% of all the displaced workers indicated that they were smoking more; 10% reported that they were drinking more as a result of displacement. Men were more likely than women to have increased their alcohol consumption (17 vs. 5%, respectively). Age and current employment status were unrelated to smoking and drinking.

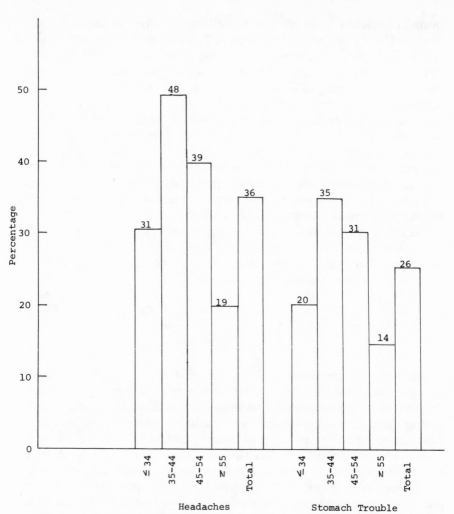

Figure 5.1. Percentage of displaced workers who reported experiencing physical symptoms due to layoff from RCA, by age categories (*N* = 324).

Mental Health

As in the case of studies of physical health, research on the effects of unemployment on mental health has yielded mixed results. Among workers displaced by the closing of two midwestern plants, there were no trends in scores on psychological indicators for a period of 2 years after the shutdown (Kasl and Cobb, 1979). The authors concluded that job loss and unemployment had effects which were limited in both magnitude and in duration on middle-aged blue-collar men's mental health.

Similarly, another longitudinal study of the effects of a plant closing on blue-collar men found relatively mild long-term psychological impact (Buss and Redburn, 1983). Specifically, on each of twelve mental health scales, unemployed steel workers "showed more stress symptoms than those who had found new jobs, were retired, or were continuously employed" (Buss and Redburn, 1983, p. 71). However, 1 year after the closing, for only four scales—increased alcohol consumption, experience of family problems, felt victimization and felt anxiousness— were scores significantly different. By the time of the second wave of the study at 2 years after the closing, these scale scores were not significantly different.

In contrast to findings of the plant closing studies just mentioned is a study of blue-collar workers whose unemployment was due largely to layoffs rather than to plant shutdowns (Liem and Liem, 1979). This study found that among married men, the unemployed had higher levels of psychiatric symptoms than a control group of employed men, at 1 month and especially at 4 months after job loss. Men reemployed by the fourth month after initial job loss showed lower levels of psychiatric symptoms than controls for five of nine symptom clusters; namely, depression, anxiety, hostility, paranoia, and somaticism.

Another relevant study concerned disruption of work life for an urban group who had been fired, laid off, demoted, or disabled due to illness (Pearlin *et al.*, 1981). Such work disruption as well as increased economic strain was related to increased depression over a 4-year period. Diminished perception of mastery over one's fate and conception of self-esteem, which resulted from both job disruption and economic strain, were also related to an increase in depression. Emotional supports and coping strategies had indirect influence on depression by reducing economic strain and by helping to maintain a sense of mastery. The mediating functions of social supports and coping strategies benefited the job losers more than those who had been stably employed.

In perhaps the only study to systematically compare blue-collar women and men's mental health effects from a U. S. plant closing, Snyder and Nowak (1984) found that between 1 and 2 years after a shutdown, unemployed men were more demoralized than reemployed men. (Demoralization was measured by the 27 questions which make up the Psychiatric Epidemiology Research Inventory or PERI.) Reemployed men with lower present wages relative to their pre-shutdown wages were more demoralized than reemployed men with higher relative wages. On the other hand, reemployed women were as demoralized as unemployed women and relative wages did not affect their demoralization.

Poor health, severity and extent of cutbacks in expenses, percentage of savings spent, and living singly with children or parents were statistically significant predicators in a regression equation to account for demoralization. Once these major determinants, many of which were gender-linked, were taken into account, gender itself did not help to explain demoralization (Snyder and Nowak, 1984).

Two other studies of general unemployment, not plant closings, found that unemployment was related to mental health for both women and men. In the Schlozman (1979, p. 307) research, comparable percentages of unemployed men and women reported being "dissatisfied with life as a whole." However, among the unemployed who were main wage earners with children, a greater percentage of women than men indicated such dissatisfaction with their lives. In the Warren (1978) study, a larger percentage of unemployed women (33%) indicated symptoms such as headache, tension, depression or insomnia than employed women (18%) and unemployed men (10%) and employed men (10%).

As indicated in the previous chapter, older workers may encounter longer periods of unemployment because of less formal education, less transferable skills, and age discrimination (Gordus, 1984; Lipsky, 1979). It has been suggested that middle-aged workers may lose social status by their inability to make the transfer from the position of "qualified worker" to "senior worker." They may also have the largest families to support and the highest incomes to lose as a result of unemployment (Brenner, 1973). Economic deprivation, in particular, is expected to lessen displaced workers' psychological well-being (Gordus *et al.*, 1981). One study which compared older to younger displaced workers, found that the older workers experienced lower levels of psychological well-being (Warren, 1978).

Findings regarding the psychological impact of reemployment following an unemployment experience are inconsistent. Studies by Aiken *et al.* (1968) and Palen (1969) indicated that improved well-being did not result from reemployment. On the other hand, Buss and Redburn (1983) found that among five groups of workers (i.e., the unemployed, those who had found new jobs, those rehired, retired, or continuously employed) the unemployed were most depressed; the rehired had the least feelings of helplessness. Similarly, Warr (1978) found that for redundant British steelworkers, those still unemployed reported lower well-being than those who were reemployed.

Additional aspects of psychological well-being include perceptions of having social support from family and friends, mastery over life, and optimism about the future. They can also be considered as moderating factors between unemployment and depression among displaced workers. Some research, for example, indicated a moderation effect of social support vis-à-vis unemployment, an effect which was stronger for psychological than for physiological variables (Liem and Liem, 1979, p. 362).

It appears that sources of support differ for women versus men. For example, in two studies unemployed women were less likely than men to seek help from their spouses, but were more likely than men to turn to other family members, friends, and neighbors (Rayman, 1982, p. 329; Warren, 1978, pp. 96–97). The data are mixed, however, regarding whether women (Rayman) or men (Warren) were more likely to maintain ties with former co-workers. Whether social support, from whatever source, has a moderating effect for unemployed women remains to be examined.

Mastery, or a feeling of control over one's future, is a personal resource which lessens the relationship between economic strain (i.e., perception of inability to afford important household items) and emotional stress (Pearlin and Schooler, 1978). Among an urban sample, men scored higher on mastery than did women, and younger people scored higher than older ones.

One coping response to economic strain is having optimistic faith in one's economic future (Pearlin and Schooler, 1978). Women are less likely than men to use this particular coping response, and older people were less likely than younger ones to use it.

RCA Findings

Social support, in the form of love and support from family and friends, varied little between the displaced RCA workers and the comparison group of continuously employed workers. Fifty-seven percent of the former and 65% of the latter reported having "lots of love and support." For the displaced, there was no difference between men and women in the percentage who perceived that they received "lots of love and support." There were also no sex differences in the level of social support for either single or married displaced workers. In addition, perception of having social support did not vary by age of workers.

To measure mastery, or a feeling of control over life, we asked the unemployed workers how strongly they agreed or disagreed with seven questions[1] developed by Pearlin and associates (1981) such as the following:

There is really no way I can solve some of the problems I have.

There is little I can do to change many of the important things in my life.

On this measure of mastery, there was a statistically significant difference between the displaced workers and the comparison sample of continuously employed workers. Summary scores for the former averaged 19, and for the latter, 21. There was a possible range of 7–28 (7 representing low mastery, and 28 high mastery).

For the displaced workers, there was no difference in sense of mastery between men and women, whether single or married, and among age groups. Moreover, the reemployed workers had no greater sense of mastery than those still unemployed.

Overall, the displaced workers were not optimistic about their economic future. Sixty-four percent disagreed with the following statement: "There is a good job waiting for me if I just look harder to find it." Women were as pessimistic as men, regardless of their marital status. Age, also, was unrelated to economic outlook. Those reemployed, however, were somewhat more optimistic about their economic futures than those who were still unemployed.

As indicated above, one of the more insidious consequences of job loss is the individuals' depression about the situation in which they find themselves. Depressed people may be unable to learn how to cope with their problems and may not take advantage of whatever opportunities are available. Thus, we asked RCA workers and the comparison group of continuously employed workers to respond to nine questions developed by Pearlin *et al.* (1981). In addition, the responses from a 1972–1973 study of a general sample of 2,300 people, ages 18–65, from the Chicago metropolitan area are reported in Table 5.1 (Pearlin

[1]The full set of statements to which respondents were asked to reply "strongly agree," "agree," "disagree," or "strongly disagree" were: (1) there is really no way I can solve some of the problems I have; (2) sometimes I feel that I'm being pushed around in life; (3) I have little control over the things that happen to me; (4) I can do just about anything I really set my mind to; (5) I often feel helpless in dealing with the problems in life; (6) what happens to me in the future mostly depends on me; and (7) there is little I can do to change many of the important things in my life.

Table 5.1. Percentage Responses to Depression Scale Items

	Very Often			Somewhat Often			Not Often/Never		
	General Sample	Employed Workers	Displaced RCA Workers	General Sample	Employed Workers	Displaced RCA Workers	General Sample	Employed Workers	Displaced RCA Workers
Lack enthusiasm for doing anything	3.3	4.8	29.3	7.2	61.9	37.1	89.4	33.3	33.6
Feel lonely	2.4	17.5	27.5	3.1	22.5	34.8	94.4	60.0	37.7
Feel bored or have little interest in doing things	2.0	9.8	37.7	3.9	46.3	31.0	94.1	43.9	31.3
Lose sexual interest/pleasure	3.6	7.5	19.3	3.6	12.5	29.1	92.8	80.0	51.7
Have trouble getting to sleep or staying asleep	2.8	12.5	38.8	4.5	25.0	27.8	92.7	62.5	33.4
Cry easily or feel like crying	2.4	7.5	19.2	2.8	10.0	29.4	94.7	82.5	51.4
Feel downhearted or blue	2.4	5.0	30.4	3.2	35.0	36.1	94.4	60.0	33.5
Feel low in energy or slowed down	2.9	10.0	28.5	4.5	50.0	43.0	92.6	40.0	28.5
Feel hopeless about the future	1.5	5.0	38.2	1.9	42.5	31.5	96.6	52.5	30.3

and Schooler, 1978; L. I. Pearlin, personal communication, 1987). It is important to note that it is among the displaced workers that the highest percentage experience every single one of these indicators "very often." The general sample has the lowest percentage experiencing these indicators "very often." The highest percentage of the displaced workers reporting any problem as occurring "very often" is thirty-nine, compared to 18% for the continuously employed and 4% for the general sample.

Comparing the displaced workers and those continuously employed, there are a number of striking differences in the percentage of each group experiencing the individual depression indicators very often. The largest was reported on the item, "During the past week, how often did you feel hopeless about the future?" There was a difference of 33%, with only 5% of the continuously employed workers in contrast to 38% of the displaced workers reporting feeling hopeless very often.

Over one-third of the former RCA workers also responded "very often" to two other items:

> *During the past week, how often did you have trouble getting to sleep or staying asleep?*

> *During the past week, how often did you feel bored or have little interest in doing things?*

In both of these cases, the percentages of the displaced workers responding "very often" exceed those of the continuously employed by more than twenty points.

Together the individual questions formed a nine-item scale, with a possible range of scores from 9 to 27. A higher score indicated higher depression. As expected, the displaced RCA workers' level of depression was greater, on the average, than that of the comparison group—scores of 17.2 versus 13.7, respectively. Moreover, responses from the general sample, cited above, evidenced an overall mean depression score of 9.8, even lower than that of the comparison group.

When the comparison group of continuously employed workers' scores were disaggregated by gender, women indicated greater depression than men (15.8 vs. 12.6, respectively). In contrast there was only a slight difference between the depression levels of the unemployed women and men (17.6 vs. 16.8).[2]

[2]These mean scores indicate that of the four groups employed men are least depressed and unemployed women are most depressed. While the subgroup comparisons suggest a sex by employment status (continuously employed vs.

Table 5.2. Regression for Depression for Displaced RCA Workers
(N = 328)

Independent Variable	Unstandardized Coefficient	Standardized Coefficient	Significance
Current employment status	.54	.07	NS
Cutbacks	−.23	−.20	.001
Mastery	.58	.37	.001
Social support	−1.05	−.14	.01
Economic optimism	−.20	−.03	NS
Gender	−.39	−.03	NS
Age	.03	.06	NS
Marital status	.11	.01	NS
Education	−.17	−.05	NS
Constant	11.21		
R^2	.30		

For displaced RCA workers, moreover, being married was no protection from depression. When we subdivided each gender by marital status, we found that unmarried men and women had similar depression scores, 18.2 and 17.9, on the average, scores which indicated only slightly greater depression than that for married men and women (16.4 and 17.4, respectively).

In addition, reemployment elsewhere did not significantly lessen the depression experienced by displacement from RCA, for either men or women. Age, on the other hand, was inversely related to depression; the older individuals had lower scores than younger ones.

We concluded our data analysis regarding depression with an assessment of the collective influence of nine previously discussed economic, social, and psychological variables on the mental health of displaced RCA workers. Specifically, in our multiple regression equation, the independent variables were current employment status, number of expense cutbacks, mastery, social support, optimism about one's economic future, gender, age, marital status, and educational attainment of respondent.

Three of the nine variables were significantly related to depression (see Table 5.2). As expected, the economic variable of cutbacks was

---

displaced) interaction, a two-way analysis of variance indicated that only the main effects were statistically significant; that is, there was no significant interaction effect.

significantly related to depression; the greater the number of cutbacks, the greater the depression. Once again, current employment status, whether unemployed or reemployed, was not significantly related to depression. Of three potentially moderating factors, a sense of mastery, perception of social support, and optimism about one's economic future, two influenced depression. One of these, a sense of mastery, was the single most influential variable in the equation. The higher one's sense of mastery, the less one's depression. Similarly, perceived social support from family and friends was negatively related to depression. None of the four remaining variables, gender, age, marital status, and educational attainment, significantly impacted on depression net of other variables in the equation. Overall, the amount of variance explained by these variables was 30%.

Family Effects

Although unemployment is usually discussed in individual terms, economic and psychological effects can extend to the whole family. Among unemployed men, a decrease in family cohesion and an increase in family tension has been found (Liem and Rayman, 1982; Schlozman, 1979).

In a study which compared unemployed men and women, more men reported increased family tension since job loss: 50 vs. 35% (Schlozman, 1979). A study of displacement by a plant closing, however, found that the decrease in marital happiness and family cohesion and adaptability was comparable for families of female and male workers (Perrucci and Targ, 1987). Moreover, these family relationships were no better for the reemployed workers than for those still unemployed.

RCA Findings

Overall, most of the former RCA workers reported that financial pressures since the shutdown had caused little change in the quality of their relationships with their spouse, children, other family members, or friends. Of the four categories of relationships, the most change occurred for marriages. Nearly one-third (31.7%) of our respondents indicated that their relationship with their spouse had worsened from financial pressures of unemployment.

Several members of the Workers Aid Council, who listened to the problems of former RCA workers, mentioned conflict between husbands and wives as a result of the plant closing. One WAC member stated the problems this way:

> Well, they're home together 24 hours a day, 24 hours a day they're at each other's throat. "Why can't you do this?" "Why can't you take out the trash?" "Why can't you get off your butt and get a job and you don't do anything around here and I have to do it all." It's just too much togetherness. And that'll do it.

A number of WAC members also mentioned separations and divorces as a result of the plant closing.

> Well you have to feel sorry for them. As long as they've got a job it worked out . . . it's not because you don't love your loved one now, it's just because the big letdown of maybe $84 . . . a week when you're used to $300 and you got this big house payment—it's a lot on our mind, and I just think that's what caused a lot of marriages to break up. . . .

For only one category of relationships, those with family other than spouse or children, did effects differ for displaced women versus men. Specifically, men were more likely than women to indicate that their extended family relationships had worsened. Single men were particularly likely to report deterioration of extended family relationships, but sex differences within marital status were not statistically significant. In addition, current employment status of the displaced workers was not related to changes in relationships with family and friends. The lack of a relationship may have been due to the reduced income and continued economic hardship of the reemployed RCA workers.

In contrast, age was related to change in quality of all categories of relationships. The younger workers (under 44) were more likely to experience deterioration, whereas older workers (over 45) were more likely to undergo no change in relationships with their spouses and nuclear and extended families. Relationships with friends were more likely to change for the worse among the very youngest group (under 34) of RCA respondents, in contrast to stability in friendships for the other age groups.

Summary and Conclusions

Significant minorities of displaced RCA workers reported that they had experienced two of five health-related problems as a consequence of their layoff; namely, headaches and stomach problems. Their cigarette smoking had also increased.

Findings regarding psychological and social well-being were mixed. On the one hand, 8 months after the closing, workers generally felt no effects of financial pressure on their relationships with spouse, children, other family members and friends. Indeed, the majority perceived that they had strong social support from family and friends. In contrast, the displaced workers reported having a weaker sense of mastery over their fates and being more depressed than a comparison sample of continually employed workers at another plant in the community. Both social support and a sense of mastery decreased depression among our respondents whereas making cutbacks in expenditures increased it. Overall, the displaced workers were not optimistic about their own economic future.

Age was usually unrelated to health and psychological well-being, with the exception that older workers indicated less depression than younger ones. Older workers also experienced more stability in their relationships with family and friends.

Importantly, we found that men and women's well-being was affected comparably by the plant closing. This is consistent with the comparable adverse financial impact of the shutdown for each gender as noted in the previous chapter.

Similarly, the reemployed's well-being was generally no better than that for individuals still jobless. This, too, is consistent with the continuing financial adversity experienced as workers become reemployed in jobs offering lower wages and less income security than their pre-shutdown positions.

Based on displaced workers' perceptions and on comparisons of the displaced with continuously employed workers, we conclude that unemployment from the plant closing has adverse impact on individuals' psychological well-being. Like much extant research (Perrucci and Perrucci, 1986), moreover, our study indicates that to a significant extent it is through economic hardships that unemployment impacts on mental health.

6

UNEMPLOYMENT AND SOCIAL INTEGRATION

As indicated in the two previous chapters, unemployed workers experience many personal problems that stem from their reduced income and the difficulties of adjusting to economic deprivation and insecurity. Many of these personal problems are faced and dealt with by displaced workers and their families. These problems have been described as "private troubles" because they are experienced as personal misfortune and they are discussed within families and among friends outside of the public eye (Mills, 1959). Sometimes there is public discussion of private troubles, such as television documentaries on the plight of the unemployed or Hollywood movies about unemployed workers. And sometimes there is public discussion of private troubles when policy-oriented groups recognize that widespread individual problems have a social basis and require social solutions.

There is another way in which the unemployed worker's private troubles are drawn into the public sphere. Displaced workers still live in communities and are involved in social life just as they did when they had a job. They still have to pay the rent or mortgage, buy groceries, take their kids to Little League games, talk to neighbors, and meet people in public as they carry out the daily routines of living. Unemployed people often suffer a loss of social standing in the eyes of others with whom they have contact. There can be a loss of personal prestige that accompanies job loss and an inability to maintain a certain way of life and the social relationships that are tied up with a way of life. Losing a job means being without a productive economic role, a situation that can result in a loss of influence among friends and family. If others start treating someone differently, there may be a loss of personal worth or self-esteem that follows from the person's belief that he/she is not held in high esteem by friends or family members. As Sennett and Cobb (1972, p. 264) noted when analyzing how class inequalities affect people: "The degree of worthiness granted a person has come to be . . . a measurement of his productivity, a personal reflection of the social uses he makes of his time."

To be unemployed means to be located at the lower end of society's system of social stratification. Those in the lower strata of society have limited income, little social influence, and minimal prestige. Those who have lost jobs because of layoffs, displacement, or demotion are often said to have experienced a "slide" down the social ladder, or to be "downwardly mobile" or "skidders" (Wilensky, 1959). There has always been a keen interest in "skidders" and those in the lower social strata because they are the *casualties* of a competitive capitalist society. The reactions of those in the lower social strata to their place in the system of inequality can tell us a great deal about the social basis of order, conflict, and change. Do they react to their own low social position, and the more favored position of others, with a feeling that things are "fair," that those who have more deserve it because of superior intelligence or hard work? Do displaced workers accept their unemployment with resignation—as an unfortunate but normal feature of an economic system that is basically sound and provides the greatest good for the greatest number? Or do they respond to their situation with a sense of outrage—that things are unfair and that the system is rigged in favor of the rich and powerful? Such reactions can tell us much about the scope and depth of alienation and anger in American society. We can also learn something of the potential for different forms of social change that might develop, such as a decline in interest in conventional party politics and increased attraction to radical movements and politics.

In this study, we asked displaced workers to tell us how the experience of the plant closing had affected their feelings about their union, their community, and their government. Their answers provide a broad spectrum of reactions. Some exhibit resignation and fatalism, others show unfocused anger and a desire to strike out, and still others express a feeling of being betrayed. A small sampling of such reactions is contained in the following remarks.

First, are comments that reflect a sense of hopelessness and despair about their situation.

26-Year-Old Divorced Woman

I have taken a lot of jobs since I lost my job at RCA. And I have found that there is little I can do for the experience and education

I have. . . . waitressing is not my lifelong dream but I can find a job easier in that field than any other, so I have to do what I have to do. . . . I have no benefits and future with no light at the end of the tunnel. You survive and grow old with nothing to show except varicose veins and a smile from those who say "girl get me this" and "I thought you went home you took so long." Only 4 or 5 tables who want your undivided attention at the same time. And a government that gets 8% of the meager $2.00 per hour I get.

45-Year-Old Married Man

We are down to rock bottom and will probably have to sell the house to live or exist until I find a job here or somewhere else. I have been everywhere looking in Cass, White and Carroll counties. We have had no help at anytime except when NIPSCO was going to shut the utilities off in March and the trustee paid that $141. My sister-in-law helps us sometime with money she's saved back or with food she canned last summer. The factories have the young. I've been to all the factories.

Another type of reaction from displaced workers reflects an erosion of trust in basic social institutions and extreme cynicism concerning the moral and ethical standards followed by most people.

32-Year-Old Married Woman

I personally believe our country's problems lay with the dishonest persons. From the man drawing a paycheck without service given, to lawyers and Congress holding things up, stretching them out, which takes big dollars from people and business. There seems to be 1,001 middlemen in business and government and unions causing outstanding overhead. Agencies, like welfare, so big they lost track of people. They play with paper and machines and we are getting ripped off. The good old lying, stealing, cheating, drug-drunk bug is what is killing our country.

39-Year-Old Married Woman

I find that working for a company who kicks my backside out the door makes me afraid to trust anyone. I'm afraid it will be years before I get up the courage to buy a car, appliances, or anything that is on a long-term note. Regardless of how good the pay is in a new job. If we all managed our homes the way the government manages theirs we'd all be on welfare. I have a National Honor Society daughter with one more year of school. If she can't get aid there's no way she can go to school.

Anger is also among the reactions of displaced workers. Sometimes it is focused on government or corporations because of their economic role in society, but sometimes it appears to be generalized anger in search of scapegoats for their frustrations.

41-Year-Old Married Man

The government is trying to cut our wages and put their foot in the working class' and poor class' face. Yet they keep raising their wages [and] find more ways than necessary to spend the taxpayer's money. Let the utility, telephone and petroleum corporations, also the big money boys have their own way without fighting for the behalf of all the people of our country. They also let the illegal aliens take our jobs away, give them welfare, unemployment [compensation] college education at our expense; do not check them for health and social diseases. Yet they want to take all the veterans' benefits away [from those] who fought their wars for them. Government of the people, by the people, and for the people—Ha!

Finally, there are those who maintain a faith in institutions and people despite their own economic problems and job insecurity.

48-Year-Old Married Man

Losing one's job is a serious jolt to your attitude of security, preservation, and well-being. However, I feel strongly that we must look forward to hope and faith in our country and its people. Deep inside I want to believe that tough times won't last, but tough people do. This will mean a lot of sacrifice, determination, and change in those people affected by losing one's job.

These comments by displaced workers are more than just self-centered emotional statements. They are deeply felt personal feelings, that are also socially anchored. The feelings expressed by workers tell us something about themselves in relation to others, whether it be Congress, their neighbors, co-workers, elected officials, rich or poor people. The way that people relate to the groups and institutions that are beyond their small circle of family and friends is an expression of social integration—the extent to which people are "tied" to the society in which they live. Some of the displaced workers feel detached or alienated from their society because they believe no one is really concerned about people like them. Some of them are angry and want to do something about their situation. Others are angry but do not know quite what to do. And there are those who feel pain but seem not to be able to express any reaction, whether it be anger or hope. They are not detached or alienated from society. They just seem to have given up. As one worker put it: "We survive, but that is not really living."

In the remainder of this chapter we examine the patterns of social integration that exist among the displaced workers. Our interest in this matter, as noted above, stems first of all from the fact that the former RCA employees are blue-collar workers and can be viewed as members of the working class. As such, they constitute a segment of society with a possible interest in changing the social order so that their interests are better served (Parkin, 1971). A second source of our interest is found in the fact that the workers we have studied have been victims of a plant closing. They have experienced a severe economic crisis as members of a collectivity and not as isolated individuals. This experience of a shared problem that was inflicted upon them may leave them less likely to blame themselves and more likely to locate the source and solution to their discontent in existing social institutions.

We will examine the degree of social integration among displaced workers with four social characteristics than can influence reactions to the closing. They are the workers' current employment status, age, gender, and work history. A discussion of these characteristics and the rationale for their inclusion follows.

1. *Employment status.* As indicated in Chapter 4, approximately 71% of the displaced workers were still unemployed 8 months after the plant closed, about 17% were reemployed full-time, and 12% had part-time jobs. The impact of the plant closing on workers who become reemployed may differ from those who remain unemployed (Kasl and Cobb, 1979; Buss and Redburn, 1983). We want to determine, first of all, whether the reemployed retain their confidence in American institutions and belief in traditional values, or whether the experience of losing a job held for 10 or 20 years has an impact on attitudes and values in spite of reemployment. If the latter is true, the experience of unemployment will have long-term consequences that do not disappear with reemployment.

2. *Age.* Younger workers with less time invested in their job at the time of the closing may feel differently about their experience than older workers with long-term employment at RCA. The younger and older workers may not view their unemployment with the same degree of despair or sense of betrayal or anger (Schlozman and Verba, 1979). Younger workers may be more optimistic about reemployment, while older workers may see limited job opportunities for the future. On the other hand, younger workers in the early stages of family development may have more debts and face more economic hardship that older workers who are without young children and the debts incurred by younger families.

3. *Gender.* If there are different reasons why men and women work

and they have different degrees of commitment to, or identification with their jobs, then it might be expected that the impact of unemployment will differ according to gender. For example, if women are temporarily involved with work, providing a second income to supplement family income and to enable the purchase of nonessential items, then unemployment may not have psychological effects such as lowered self-esteem. Fuchs (1971) suggests that employment for women from some lower-income groups is "family-oriented," in that it is viewed as a temporary extension of the family role of women and it limits identification with the occupational role. On the other hand, women may be involved with work in ways that are similar to men, either because they are sole providers or because they prefer employment to domestic roles. If women do not derive social or psychological meaning from work, their unemployment should not have consequences that extend beyond the financial sphere. Women should be less likely than men to use the experience of unemployment to react critically and negatively to American institutions and values. For example, Schlozman and Verba (1979, p. 76) found that unemployed "housewife reentrants" into the labor force report much lower levels of dissatisfaction with their income than male workers or women who are the main wage earners. However, if women and men have similar work commitments we would expect them to experience similar psychological reactions to job loss.

4. *Work history.* Displaced RCA workers whose work history contains no prior period of unemployment may be expected to respond differently to the plant closing than workers who have had a prior period of unemployment. The experience of having faced unemployment previously might have produced a degree of cynicism about the uncertainties of the labor market that subsequently serves as a buffer against more severe psychological reactions. At the same time, the insecurity of repeated unemployment can lead to greater support for political change (Schlozman and Verba, 1979, p. 80). Those who have never experienced unemployment or an extended layoff may feel that such a thing could never happen to them and they are, therefore, less prepared for the situation and more likely to experience the stress of unemployment.

Social integration, the dependent variable, is viewed as having seven different dimensions, ranging from very specific reactions to the RCA plant closing to feelings and patterns of involvement regarding their union and community, to general attitudes and beliefs about American institutions and values. The different meanings of social integration that assess the nature of the "social bond" between unemployed workers and the larger society include responses to the following questions.

a. Why did the RCA plant close? Workers can view the RCA corporation as being entangled in economic forces which they cannot control or as making decisions that are profit-centered and anti-worker and union.

b. Which groups have the most influence on the government in Washington, D.C., and which groups should have the most influence? Workers may view their society as pluralist in nature, where different interest groups compete to influence different policies, or they may see their society as dominated by big government or big business. Preferences about how influence *should* be distributed reflects the discrepancy between "what is" and "what ought to be."

c. What do workers believe about future employment opportunities? Even though presently unemployed, workers can be optimistic about their future. Those who view their situation as temporary, reflecting short-term problems in an otherwise healthy economy, are more integrated than workers with pessimistic views of the future.

d. Do workers view their community as concerned and helpful with regard to the plight of displaced RCA workers? Unemployed workers who feel that their community's social, civic, and political groups are very concerned and supportive in their time of need are more integrated into their society than workers who feel they are facing things alone.

e. How much confidence do workers have in national social institutions and how have their views been affected by the plant closing? Workers with little confidence in national leaders and in the social institutions of society that are alleged to serve their interests are less integrated into society than workers with confidence.

f. Is there a belief in equality of opportunity for children of workers and executives? The American system of stratification has been described as having both great inequality and equality of opportunity. It is the belief in the existence of opportunity that permits inequality without class conflict. Workers who believe in the existence of equal opportunity regardless of social origins are more integrated into society than those who do not hold such a belief.

g. Do workers endorse government policies that are designed to redistribute income and provide government-sponsored job and income maintenance programs? Workers who endorse government actions that would lead to income redistribution are less integrated into society as it is currently structured and are seeking significant social change.

Comparison of Displaced Worker and Employed Workers in the Same Community

Before making comparisons among the displaced workers in their feelings of alienation from or attachment to their society, we first compare all displaced workers with other workers in the same community. The comparison group is composed of workers in another manufacturing plant with skill levels comparable to the RCA workers. Such a comparison will allow us to see if the RCA workers, in general, differ from other manual workers on the measures of social integration. If they differ, it is likely that the reasons for difference lie in experiences related to the plant closing. If the two groups of workers do not differ, it is unlikely that the plant closing had an impact on the feelings of alienation or integration among the unemployed.

A comparison of the attitudes and beliefs of displaced RCA workers with continuously employed workers from another manufacturing plant indicates that there are some similarities and some notable differences between the two groups (data not shown).[1] When asked to respond to questions about why the RCA plant closed, three-fourths or more of both groups of workers believe the decision was motivated by a desire for greater profits and an opportunity to use the recession as an excuse to break the power of unions. While the large majority of both groups hold these beliefs, they are more strongly held by the former RCA workers. Only a minority of both groups (about 20%) believe that the RCA corporation had no choice in closing the plant because of general economic conditions, or that the plant would have stayed open if the workers had agreed to make substantial wage concessions. The absence of differences in beliefs about the plant closing between displaced RCA workers and employed workers is interesting in that it indicates a substantial core of suspicion and mistrust of the RCA corporation's motives that goes beyond the experience of being a displaced worker.

Both groups of workers were also asked to give their opinions about the relative influence exerted upon the government in Washington, D.C., by military leaders, unions, rich people, small business, big business, and the poor. In addition, they were asked to identify the groups that should have the most influence, thus permitting comparisons to be made

[1] Data are available upon request. The items for which comparative data are available include some of those listed in Table 6.2.

of what workers believe to be the actual and preferred patterns of influence. Both groups of workers overwhelmingly identify "big business" as exercising the most influence, followed by "rich people." All other groups receive very few choices as sources of influence. When expressing their preferences about who should exercise influence, both displaced and employed workers state that "all groups should be equal," with distant second choices going to "unions," "small business," and "poor people."

Perhaps the best indication of social integration among workers is provided by their views of major social institutions. Displaced workers and employed workers were asked to indicate their feelings of confidence, or lack thereof in national leaders and institutions. Respondents were presented with a list of twelve institutional areas including politics, professions, television news, unions, and business and asked to indicate whether they had "lots," "some," or "hardly any" confidence in each. The least confidence was expressed by displaced workers for national and local political leaders and institutions, and for big business (i.e., 40–50% of workers saying "hardly any" confidence). The continuously employed workers (who are non-union) have hardly any confidence in labor unions (76%), Congress (33%), and the legal profession (31%). There are statistically significant differences between displaced and employed workers' confidence in American leaders and institutions for eight of the twelve institutional areas considered. There are no differences between the two groups of workers in terms of their confidence in religious institutions, television news shows, schools, and the legal profession.

It is also interesting to compare feelings of confidence in institutions for displaced RCA workers and employed non-union workers in Monticello, and a general sample of the American public. In the previous paragraph we compared the percentage of workers stating that they had "hardly any confidence" in selected institutions. We now compare group differences in the percentage stating they have a "great deal of confidence" in institutions.

Table 6.1 provides a summary of information on confidence in institutions for two national opinion polls (1966 and 1984) and for the two samples of workers from Monticello (employed and displaced RCA workers). Both groups of workers from Monticello have substantially less confidence in social institutions than a national sample of Americans. Employed workers from Monticello are similar to the average American in a number of areas, and displaced RCA workers have the least confidence in institutions of the four groups that are compared.

Table 6.1. Percentage Expressing "A Great Deal of Confidence"
in Institutions [a]

	National Poll Data		Employed RCA Workers in Monticello (1984)	Displaced RCA Workers in Monticello (1984)
	1966	1984		
Medical profession	72	43	41	34
Education (schools*)	61	40	24*	24*
Legal profession	—	—	14	10
Military	62	45	—	—
Presidency	41	42	36	10
Religious institutions	41	24	24	27
Supreme court	50	35	21	10
Major corporations (big business*)	55	19	5*	3*
Labor Unions	22	12	2	22
Congress	42	28	2	3
Press (TV news shows*)	29	18	12*	15*
State legislature	—	—	7	4
Governor	—	—	14	6
Average percentage with "great deal of confidence" across all institutions	48	31	17	13

[a] Asterisks refer to differences in wording of questionnaires in the different polls.

Source: 1966 Poll Data: Lipset and Schneider (1983); 1984 Poll Data: Lou Harris Poll.

In fact, the overall level of confidence across all institutions expressed by displaced workers suggests a legitimacy crisis of substantial proportion.

These findings indicate that while displaced workers express a considerable lack of confidence in social institutions, especially those involving political leaders and business, this expression of alienation does not extend with the same negative force to other institutions such as education, religion, and medicine. These latter groups are probably viewed as less directly involved in the cause or solution of high unemployment. However, the degree of confidence expressed in these institutions is modest and unenthusiastic.

The final indicator of social integration is reflected in workers' belief in a generalized value usually called the "American Dream," the existence of equality of opportunity for all persons regardless of their social origins. Respondents were asked whether children of a factory worker had the same chance, somewhat less chance, or much less chance of getting ahead than children of an executive. One-third of displaced RCA workers compared to 17% of employed workers said that workers' children had "much less" chance.

These data comparing displaced workers and employed workers on various indicators of social integration indicate that the displaced workers express more feelings of alienation from society. Since we do not have pre- and post-plant closing measures for the RCA workers, comparisons with employed workers provide greater confidence that the expressions of alienation are related to the unemployment experience.

Comparisons Among Displaced Workers

In this section of the chapter we examine the effects of current employment status, history of unemployment, gender, and age upon a number of different indicators of social integration. In general, we will describe the findings obtained in our analysis without reporting the data in tables or graphs. A summary of findings is reported in Table 6.2.

Employment Status

Displaced workers who are reemployed after the closing do not differ from those who are continuously unemployed in their beliefs about why the RCA plant closed. Neither group is inclined to be either more critical (e.g., "union busting") or more understanding (e.g., "no choice, given the foreign competition") of RCA's decision to close the plant. The two groups also do not differ in their feelings of confidence in social institutions as a result of the plant closing, or in their feelings about whether the local community or state officials did much to help the displaced RCA workers.

When questioned about their views of future employment opportunities, employed and unemployed displaced workers expressed opin-

**Table 6.2. Summary of Relationships between Worker Characteristics
and Social Integration**[a]

	Employment Status	Previous Unemployment	Gender	Age
Causes of unemployment				
1. Why did RCA close?				
A. No choice; foreign competition	NS	NS	NS	NS
B. Union busting; more profits	NS	*	NS	NS
C. Union reluctance to cut wages	NS	NS	NS	*
Community-institutional support				
2. Community support for workers since plant closed	NS	NS	NS	NS
3. Confidence in social institutions	NS	NS	*	NS
4. Confidence in institutions since plant closing	NS	NS	NS	*
Opportunity structure				
5. What are future employment prospects?				
A. Good jobs are available; must look harder	*	NS	NS	*
B. Impossible to find a job, no matter what I do	*	*	NS	*
C. Getting a job is all luck	NS	NS	NS	NS
D. Jobs will come when economy picks up	*	NS	NS	*
E. Will find new job even if economy doesn't pick up	*	*	NS	*
6. Opportunities for children of workers and executives	NS	*	NS	NS

(continued)

Table 6.2. *Continued*

	Employment Status	Previous Unemploy- ment	Gender	Age
Egalitarian change				
7. Do you support these government policies?				
A. Government as employer of displaced workers	NS	NS	NS	*
B. Guaranteed family income	*	*	NS	NS
C. Reduce taxes on business	NS	NS	NS	NS
D. Higher taxes on rich and redistribute wealth	NS	*	NS	NS
E. Limit incomes	NS	NS	NS	NS
F. Reduce size of government	NS	NS	*	*

[a]NS, Not significant; * = significant at $p \leq .05$.

ions reflecting different degrees of optimism or pessimism. Displaced workers who found new employment were more likely to believe that a "good job was waiting for them" and that they would find a good job even if the economy did not improve. In contrast, over 60% of displaced workers who are continuously unemployed believe that it will be impossible to find a job in the future, compared to one-third of the employed workers who hold this pessimistic view. These differences between employed and unemployed workers displaced by the plant closing are not surprising. Those who are fortunate enough to find a new job after the closing would be expected to believe that the future would hold additional opportunities, while those who are continuously unemployed would be more pessimistic.

Both employed and unemployed displaced workers were also questioned about their views of the opportunity structure for young people; that is, how did they compare the chances of success for the child of a factory worker with the child of a business executive. No difference was found between these groups in their belief in equality of opportunity, often referred to as the "American Dream."

Finally, workers were questioned about their support for, or opposition to, specific government actions on economic policies relevant to workers and the business community. The actions involved (a) government employment programs for the unemployed, (b) providing a guaranteed income for all families, (c) reducing taxes on business in order to stimulate the economy, (d) raising taxes of the rich in order to redistribute wealth, (e) establishing limits on top levels of income, and (f) reducing the size of government. Unemployed and employed displaced workers differed only on the question of establishing a guaranteed income. The continuously unemployed workers were more likely to endorse such a line of action.

In summary, the most notable finding is the small number of significant differences between employed and unemployed displaced workers on the measures of social integration. Only the questions related to future employment opportunities revealed differences according to workers' current employment status, but these are to be expected. This suggests that the experience of the plant closing has effects on workers that endure despite their having been reemployed. Both unemployed and reemployed workers reveal similar levels of distrust and pessimism about their society. How long such negative effects will continue to be experienced for both reemployed and continuously unemployed workers is unknown. What is known is that reemployment alone is not sufficient to eliminate the lack of social integration that accompanies unemployment due to a plant closing.

Work History

Displaced RCA workers who have experienced prior periods of unemployment were compared with those lacking such experiences on the different measures of social integration. Those who had experienced unemployment earlier in their work history are more likely to (a) believe that the RCA plant was a profitable operation, but that it closed in order to increase profits, (b) be pessimistic about their future employment opportunities, (c) support a government policy to provide a guaranteed income, and (d) support government action to raise taxes to the rich in order to redistribute wealth. Contrary to expectations, workers with prior unemployment experience (27%) are somewhat more likely than workers without prior unemployment (16%) to believe that the child of a factory worker has the same chance as does the child of a business executive to get ahead.

These two groups of displaced workers do not differ on their confidence in national and local institutions, their beliefs about who does and should exercise influence in Washington, and their beliefs about how much help the local community provided to displaced workers after the closing.

Gender

Very few differences are found between men and women workers on the various measures of social integration. Women workers differ from men on only two items: (a) women are more likely to express greater confidence in American social institutions, and (b) women are less likely than men (14 vs. 26%) to feel that the size of government should be reduced even if it means cutting back on government services in health and education.

The virtual absence of differences between men and women workers on these measures of social integration leads to the conclusion that the gender status of displaced RCA workers does not differentially affect their response to the plant closing in terms of feelings of alienation from or integration into their society. These findings do not lend support to the hypothesis that unemployment has a lesser impact on women workers because they are less committed to or involved in work or because they do not need to work.

Age

The fourth and final worker characteristic examined in relation to social integration is age. Displaced workers are grouped into four age categories: 19–29, 30–39, 40–49, and 50 or more years of age. The groupings correspond to different amounts of work experience and different stages of the life cycle. They reflect different levels of financial security, work career development, and hopes for the future. Very little is known about how chronological age and work career stage mediates the unemployment experience. Plausible hypotheses are that the youngest workers would have the easiest time adapting to unemployment because they have made less of an investment in their jobs and probably have fewer financial obligations (e.g., home mortgage, older children). Workers in the two middle age brackets might experience more financial strain but should more easily be able to convert their work experience into a new job. Older workers might be in better shape financially because their large investments in homes or cars are behind them, and their children no longer represent a financial problem. However, older workers should have more pessimistic views about future job opportunities. Some representative comments by older workers make some of these points clearly.

52-Year-Old Married Woman

At my age I doubt I would ever find a decent paying job. And as long as there are family men who need a job it would not be fair for me to accept one when I am not the only source of income.

61-Year-Old Married Woman

I have put my application in three places, but they don't have anyone at the age 60. In fact, they don't ask your age or birth date; they ask you when you graduated from high school. So what does that tell you?

50-Year-Old Single Man

At my age I feel like it's almost too late to start over.

One can see from summary Table 6.2 that a worker's age is significantly related to more measures of social integration than was the case for employment status, work history, or gender. Looking first at workers' beliefs about why the RCA plant closed (Figure 6.1), it appears that the youngest workers (19–29 years of age) are the least likely to agree with statements that could be viewed as critical of RCA's decision to close. The youngest workers are less likely to agree with the statements that: "The Monticello plant was probably making money, but not as much as it could if it moved to a lower wage area," and "RCA used the excuse of the recession to break the back of organized labor and get lower wages." However, these differences are not statistically significant. They are significantly more likely to believe that "RCA would have kept the plant open if the union would have agreed to large cuts in wages and benefits."

Older workers (40–49 and 50 and over) are more likely than younger workers to endorse statements that could be interpreted as critical of RCA. There is the belief among older workers that RCA was interested in greater profits and "breaking the back" of labor. These older age groups also did not agree that RCA would have remained open if workers agreed to large wage cuts.

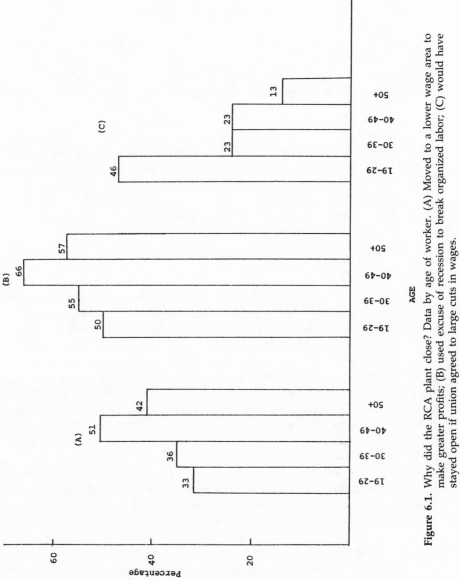

Figure 6.1. Why did the RCA plant close? Data by age of worker. (A) Moved to a lower wage area to make greater profits; (B) used excuse of recession to break organized labor; (C) would have stayed open if union agreed to large cuts in wages.

These statements about why RCA closed the Monticello plant reflect what workers were saying and thinking right after the plant closed. During the first few months of field observation and informal interviews with workers, it was clear to the researchers that the most militant anti-RCA workers believed that the plant closing was in the planning stage for a long time. A new RCA plant in a non-union area in a Southern state was believed to be the new production location for the cabinets formerly manufactured in Monticello. Militant workers also believed that no amount of "give-back" in wages and benefits would have prevented the closing. They frequently pointed out that the union had agreed to a 30% reduction in wages and benefits and that RCA had rejected the offer. Many pro-union workers believed that the negotiations over different "give-back" plans was a smoke screen to make it appear as if RCA would consider staying if the union was more reasonable in its wage demands. It was also believed to be a strategy to maintain productivity while making preparations to close.

Given the prevailing beliefs in some worker circles about why the RCA plant closed, the noncritical stance of younger workers is interesting. It probably reflects a lesser commitment to union solidarity or a belief that as the youngest workers they are most vulnerable to job loss and that the union cannot protect them during hard times. Whatever the source of the beliefs of younger workers, they present a special challenge to organized labor.

Displaced workers of different ages hold varying beliefs about future employment opportunities. All workers were asked to respond to five questions concerning how they viewed their prospects for employment in the future. Responses to these questions can be considered to reflect two underlying dimensions; the first involves optimism-pessimism, and the second involves the extent to which the chances of finding a job are under the control of the worker.

Figure 6.2 contains the data on how workers of different ages responded to four of the questions about future employment.[2] There is a general pattern in the responses indicating that younger workers are both more optimistic about their future employment opportunities and feel that they have more control over their situation. Looking at the first two questions we can see that the percentage of workers agreeing that they can find a job if they look harder declines gradually with increasing age. Only 10% of the oldest age group agrees with the state-

---

[2]The fifth question was "Finding a job is a matter of luck." Between 50 and 60% of the displaced workers agreed with this question, but the responses of the different age groups were not statistically significant.

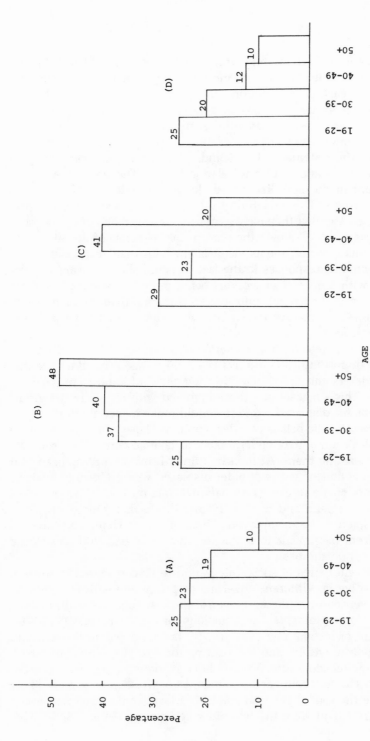

Figure 6.2. Beliefs about future employment of age of worker (percentage agreeing with each statement). (A) Good job waiting for me if I look harder; (B) No matter what I do, impossible to find a job; (C) When the economy picks up I will find a job easily; (D) Will find a job even if the economy doesn't pick up.

ment. Responses to the statement that despite individual effort, "it will be impossible to find a job" are more sharply related to age. Younger workers are least likely to endorse this pessimistic forecast, while each successive age group gives greater endorsement.

The last two questions provide an indication of how workers see their employment prospects in relation to the general economy. Responses to the statement "I will find a job when the economy picks up" reveal an erratic pattern in relation to age. The 40- to 49-year-old workers are much more likely to endorse this statement than any of the other groups. This may reflect the optimism of experienced workers who may feel that they have a lot to offer, but that a growing economy is necessary. Whatever the reason, the response of the 40–49 age group to this question seems inconsistent with their responses to the other questions. Responses to the last question show a clear age relationship, with the younger workers being more optimistic and having a greater sense of personal control of the situation than the older workers. Responses to the last question have a pattern that is very similar to the first question.

It is clear, therefore, that workers' optimism about their future employment opportunities is indirectly related to age. The older the displaced workers the less "rosy" is their view of future employment prospects. This suggests that those involved with retraining programs or job clubs for displaced workers should make a special effort to deal with the pessimistic beliefs of older workers. Those who see the future in such bleak terms may be less likely to take advantage of programs aimed at assisting them. At the same time, it must be recognized that the more pessimistic views of older displaced workers may be realistic assessments of the future, since national data on reemployment cited in Chapter 5 (Flaim and Sehgal, 1985) indicate that younger workers are more likely to be reemployed. Thus, efforts to change attitudes of workers from pessimistic to optimistic should be tied to the existence of real job opportunities.

The final measures of social integration to be considered in relation to age involve six different government policy alternatives including (a) the government as the employer of those without jobs, (b) income maintenance programs, (c) tax reductions for big business, (d) limits on the amount of income one can earn, (e) tax increases on the rich and redistribution of wealth, and (f) reducing the size of government. There are few age-related differences in how workers responded to these questions. The two younger age categories of workers were more likely to endorse the role of government as employer of those without work (54 and 51%) than were the two older age groups (34 and 39%). This seems surprising since the concept of government as employer of last resort during "hard times" (e.g., WPA projects of the 1930s) might be more familiar to older workers.

The second policy for which there are age differences involves the suggestion that the size of government should be reduced, even if it means a reduction in government services in the areas of health and education. The oldest age group was most supportive of reducing the size of government, a position that is consistent with their opposition to having the government be the employer of last resort. Those most opposed to reducing the size of government were 19-to 29- and 40-to 49-year-old workers. Thus, there is an erratic pattern to the way that age of workers may influence their view of government policy.

We conclude this section on differences in social integration among displaced workers with the generalization that the gender of workers and their current employment status had the least effect on workers' alienation from or integration into their society. These are important findings in that they add support to a growing body of research indicating that women's involvement in the work force is more similar than different from that of men. They also indicate that the impact of the plant closing on workers' feelings of social integration are not altered by being reemployed.

A second generalization to be drawn from this section is that a worker's age and experience of prior unemployment have the greatest impact on displaced workers' feelings of social integration/alienation.

Levels of Social Integration and Its Correlates

Up to this point we have looked at social integration in terms of separate and discrete attitudes and beliefs about social institutions, perceptions of the opportunity structure, and similar measures of the strength of the social bond. We now look at the relationship among these separate indicators of social integration to see if it is possible to think of "levels" of social integration. The level of integration refers to the social and temporal location of the experience or idea that is the object of a worker's positive or negative reaction. For example, when thinking about why the RCA plant closed workers are dealing with a personal experience that has recently occurred. Similarly, when discussing their feelings about help received from people and groups in their community they are dealing with concrete experiences that are currently taking place. However, when workers are asked about future job opportunities or beliefs about equality of opportunity or the need for social change they are referring to abstract ideas or things that might possibly occur in the future. Thus, levels of integration range from reactions to personal experiences and local community conditions to feelings about groups that are more remote from their everyday lives (e.g., the Supreme Court) and abstract values. We wish to see if the feelings of integration directed toward workers' personal and local experiences are consistent with or different from those directed toward more remote objects.

Figure 6.3 provides a graphic illustration of different levels of social integration as a series of concentric circles or zones of experience. At the center of the diagram is the question of why the RCA plant closed. We assume that this is an experience of great significance in the lives of the workers. Its impact is immediate, profound, and far-reaching, as it altered established and stable relationships between workers, their union, the community, and RCA. We further assume that the way that

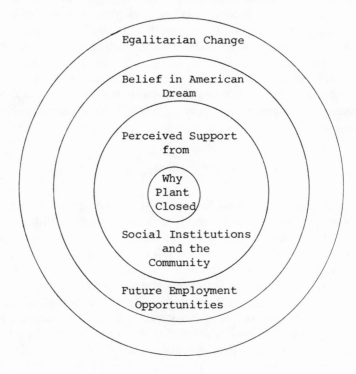

Figure 6.3. Levels of social integration.

people "explain" to themselves why the plant closed can have consequences for other social and political beliefs and attitudes.

The second circle from the center in Figure 6.3 involves workers'
perception of how much support they received from the local community and state officials in relation to the plant closing, and the feelings
of loss of confidence in social institutions because of the plant closing.
In this "level of experience" we assume that displaced workers develop
a feeling about whether "anybody out there" is aware of what happened to them and willing to help. In field observations we encoun-
tered numerous situations in which workers made clear distinctions
between agencies and between people (e.g., political officials, clergy,
social service directors) who were concerned about the plight of displaced workers and helpful to them, and those who were indifferent.

The third concentric circle involves workers' feelings about their future prospects. At the level of direct relevance to workers is the matter
of future employment opportunities. At a more abstract level, workers
may think differently about basic values like the so-called American
Dream. We assume that for some workers the plant closing experience
will provide a challenge to long-held values about America as the land
of opportunity for people who are willing to work; others may respond
to the closing as an unfortunate and unavoidable problem, but only a
temporary setback.

The outer circle concerns the possible consequences of what workers
confronted in each of the other zones of experience. One possible consequence concerns the belief that some form of *social change* is necessary to help remedy the problems experienced by displaced workers.
We assume that most displaced workers had to decide on what individual changes they and their families would have to make in order to
cope with unemployment. They may have changed eating habits, family schedules, and relationships with friends as ways of coping. But do
they consider changes outside of themselves as possible remedies? Do
they think that the actions of government should be different in order
to remedy the problems of displaced workers, or to prevent future plant
closings?

In order to see how the different levels of social integration are interrelated we first obtained summary indexes of questions reflecting
the levels of experience in Figure 6.3. The summary indexes for each
level are as follows.[3]

---

[3]Reliability coefficients for the multi-item indexes were computed using
Cronbach's Alpha. The Alpha for community support was .89; for confidence
in institutions before the closing, .79; for confidence in institutions after the

Level A: (1) Beliefs about why RCA closed.
Level B: (2) Perceptions of support from local community.
        (3) Confidence in social institutions before the plant clos-
        ing.
        (4) Confidence in social institutions after the plant closing.
Level C: (5) Perception of future employment opportunities
        (6) Beliefs about chances to get ahead for child of factory
        worker and business executive.
Level D: (7) Attitudes toward government policies aimed at egali-
        tarian change.

The seven summary indexes from the four levels of experience are intercorrelated in order to locate patterns of consistent or inconsistent reactions by displaced workers. The seven indexes are also correlated with four worker characteristics that could influence beliefs, perceptions, and attitudes. They are worker's age, gender, present employment status, and previous unemployment experience (the same characteristics contained in Table 6.1).

Table 6.3 presents the correlations among the seven indexes of social integration and four worker characteristics. Starting with beliefs about why RCA closed, there are two significant correlations. Workers who are less critical of RCA for closing the plant have high confidence in social institutions and they are less likely to endorse government policies aimed at egalitarian change.

In the second level of experience, displaced workers' perceptions of community support and confidence in social institutions are highly interrelated. Workers who perceive their community as not being supportive of displaced workers also lack confidence in social institutions. These beliefs about the community and major social institutions also carry over to influence perceptions and beliefs about the future. Workers with negative feelings about their community and those lacking confidence in institutions are also more pessimistic about future employment opportunities. They are also less likely to endorse the belief that a child of a factory worker and business executive have an equal chance to succeed in America.

Only one of the indexes from the second level of experience (confidence in institutions after the closing) is tied to support for egalitarian social change. Workers whose confidence in institutions declined as a

---

closing, .83; and for future employment opportunities, .64. This indicates that responses to the individual items that make up each index were consistent and suggests that the manifest content of items is similar.

Table 6.3. Intercorrelations of Indexes of Social Integration and Worker Characteristics

	1	2	3	4	5	6	7	Age	Gender	Employment Status	Previous Employment
1. Why RCA closed		.00	.13***	.07	.04	.05	-.10**	-.00	-.01	.06	-.06
2. Community support			.21***	.29***	.13**	-.04	.04	-.00	.05	-.00	.01
3. Confidence in institutions (before)				.37***	.13**	.00	.02	-.00	-.02	.08*	-.03
4. Confidence in institutions (after)					.07*	.15**	.08*	-.06	.11**	.03	-.01
5. Future employment opportunities						-.16***	-.24***	-.17***	.11**	.20***	.11**
6. Child's chances to get ahead							.19***	.04	-.09*	.06	-.04
7. Egalitarian change								-.13**	-.01	-.06	.18***

* = $p \leq .10$
** = $p \leq .05$
*** = $p \leq .01$

result of the plant closing are more likely to support government actions to assist the unemployed and to redistribute wealth.

Both workers' feelings about their future employment opportunities and their belief in equality of opportunity are associated with their endorsement of government policies aimed at egalitarian social change. Workers who are pessimistic about their future employment, and who see the child of a factory worker as having less of a chance to get ahead than the child of a business executive, are more likely to endorse government policies aimed at egalitarian social change.

Considering the general pattern of intercorrelations among the seven indexes reflecting different levels of social integration, there are clear relationships between how workers feel in one area of experience and how they feel in another. For example, the way that displaced workers come to "explain" for themselves why the RCA plant closed is related to how they feel about their society at a more general level. Similarly, workers' feelings about their treatment in their own community has consequences for their confidence in national social institutions and their feelings about the future. Finally, workers' feelings about the future are clearly tied to their support for more radical government action to assist the unemployed and to redistribute wealth. In sum, the intercorrelations in Table 6.3 support the idea that different levels of social integration from the specific (why did RCA close?) to the general (support for radical social change) are not isolated and discontinuous feelings and beliefs. What happens to workers in one area of experience influences their feelings in other areas. Whether or not such attitudes and beliefs have consequences for behavior remains to be seen.

The final relevant data in Table 6.3 are the intercorrelations between the indexes of social integration and four worker characteristics. The strongest relationships exist between belief about future employment opportunities and each of the four worker characteristics. This is followed by endorsement of egalitarian social change, which is correlated with age and previous unemployment.

The correlations between worker characteristics and the seven indexes reported in Table 6.3 may differ somewhat from those reported in Table 6.2 because (1) in Table 6.2 are reported chi-square statistics for individual items that are later combined into a summary index in Table 6.3, and (2) Table 6.3 reports Pearson correlation coefficients, which are more sensitive to the degree of linearity in the relationship between two variables. The most notable difference between Tables 6.2 and 6.3 on the significance of worker characteristics, is that gender is somewhat more strongly related to several of the summary indexes of social integration than it is with individual items that comprise the indexes.

Summary

The costs of unemployment extend far beyond the economic area of life. Displaced workers exhibit a high level of alienation and distrust of the groups and institutions that comprise the social fabric in the community and at the national level. The expressions of alienation do not appear to be isolated or limited to specific situations. Displaced workers' suspicions about why the RCA plant closed extend outward to incorporate feelings of being ignored by their community, beliefs about limited opportunities for employment in the future, and beliefs about the need for radical social change to help the unemployed and less privileged.

The expressions of alienation in the attitudes and beliefs of displaced workers are not especially influenced by workers' age, gender, current employment status, or prior unemployment experience. However, there are two notable exceptions. First, beliefs about future employment opportunities are more pessimistic for older workers, women, the continuously unemployed, and those with a history of prior unemployment. Second, support for radical social change is weakest among older workers and strongest among those who have experienced unemployment before.

7

WORKER CONSCIOUSNESS

The previous chapter focused on social integration as it is expressed in displaced workers' beliefs and attitudes about their community and society. Worker responses reflected feelings of alienation from their society, a lack of faith or confidence in social institutions, and an absence of optimism about the future. Such expressions of alienation are wide-ranging in nature and lack a focus of attention on a single form of alienation or integration. For example, workers can be alienated from national social institutions but integrated into community life.

In this chapter, we focus on a specific response of workers that goes beyond general alienation, a response to their economic crisis that reflects a new way of becoming integrated into social life. This response is worker consciousness, an awareness of the interests shared by workers and an understanding of the social and economic forces that influence them as workers.[1] In general, some workers never move beyond

---

[1]Worker consciousness is not the same as the more frequently used concept of class consciousness. The latter concept has engendered enormous debate in the literature and is perhaps best studied in historically developing circumstances. Our use of worker consciousness emphasizes the extent to which workers who are collectively experiencing a plant closing change their outlook on the state, the economy, and their own situation. Consequently, we make no claims that worker consciousness reflects identification with class-wide interests or that there exists the larger structural conditions favorable to the formation of class interests. For a fuller treatment of worker consciousness, see Simpson and Simpson (1984).

feelings of generalized alienation or unfocused anger when trying to make sense out of their situation. Others seem to give more focus to their feelings and express the outlines of an alternative way of looking at their situation. This is indicated by what some of the displaced RCA workers have to say about themselves and their problems.

36-Year-Old Single Female

I have found there is a class difference in America . . . My feeling about government has changed. Before, I paid my taxes thinking they went to help the needy, the disadvantaged, but not now. The administration that is in now thinks things should go back to the 1930s. They think there should be a class difference. Those with money should be able to divide up the pie—the world—and say who should get it.

44-Year-Old Single Female

There was a time in this country when any person willing to work hard and long enough could have a piece of the so-called American dream. But now, due to the greed of stock holders and big business wanting and demanding a bigger piece of the pie at the cost of the American workers this is no longer possible.

56-Year-Old Married Female

Big business has a hold over this entire country.

The above statements contain an awareness of class differences and an identification of business interests as a source of the problem facing workers. They are notably different from fatalistic views ("The plant closing is just a fact of life that happens occasionally; everything has to get better in time"), anti-foreigner sentiments ("The government needs to quit letting foreigners come in and take our jobs"), anti-import and anti-foreign competition opinions ("The government needs to tax imports more so the foreign products don't come to the U.S. so readily and be sold cheaper than our own products"), or self-blame ("A person gets help if they are willing to put a little effort toward helping themselves. Why blame the company or union when the people themselves didn't care about the quality of the job they did").

What distinguishes displaced workers who exhibit a higher degree of awareness of class inequality in America from those who tend not to think in such terms? Why do some displaced workers see the interests of workers as conflicting with those of management or business while others do not? Why do some displaced workers support more "radical" remedies to their problem while others rely on conventional solutions? These are the questions that concern us in this chapter.

Social Inequality and the Working Class

Students of social stratification have had a long-standing interest in the question of how people react to their position in a system of inequality. Attention has focused on the extent of peoples' awareness of the hierarchical structures in which they are embedded, their tendency to view hierarchies as composed of distinct and discontinuous strata, and their tendency to identify with others who are similarly located and to act in accordance with perceived common interests (Vanneman and Pampel, 1977).

Such foci are of central importance for understanding the forces that serve to perpetuate or change a particular system of stratification. If there is limited awareness of inequality, resignation and acceptance of inequality, and limited life chances, or successful socialization into the legitimating ideology of dominant groups, there will be few efforts by disadvantaged groups to change the social arrangements under which they labor. On the other hand, if there are organized beliefs that question the legitimacy of the existing order, and groups capable of mobilizing those beliefs, one would expect to find conditions favorable for collective political action calling for change.

Research on reactions to inequality indicates that peoples' positions in a system of inequality influence their reactions to it. For example, peoples' judgments about the fairness of earnings going to individuals and households are related to their social status (Alves and Rossi, 1978). High-status persons are more likely to base their judgments of fairness on merit, while low-status persons emphasize need when making judgments about whether incomes are fair. Rytina *et al.* (1970) found that "rich" respondents are more likely than the "poor" to believe that (1) the United States has equality of opportunity, (2) rich and poor alike can influence government, (3) there is equal access to education, and (4) wealth is the result of hard work, self-discipline, and intelligence. Finally, Jackman and Jackman (1983) found that the poor, in contrast to working class, middle class, and upper middle class, are most likely to want government to play an active role in guaranteeing jobs and a minimum income for all citizens.

Reactions to one's position in a stratification system can include a wide range of possibilities. Parkin (1971) has suggested that those least favored in a system of inequality respond either by (1) accepting the dominant value system that encourages individual achievement and legitimates inequality, (2) embracing a subordinate value system that is critical of inequality but does not advocate collective action for change, or (3) adopting a radical value system that springs from a political ideology and class-based organization.

Many of the questions about how people react to inequality are reflected in a body of scholarly work on class consciousness. Based in Marxian and conflict theorists' concerns with working class movements aimed at radical social change, the study of class consciousness has been controversial. Some have maintained that the conditions of the working class have changed so substantially that it is currently meaningless to study class conflict and class consciousness. Those who hold such views point to the disappearance of class antagonism, the institutionalization of worker-management conflict, and the rising incomes and standard of living of the working class (Dahrendorf, 1959, 1964). This has resulted in a so-called *embourgeoisement* thesis that sees blue-collar workers becoming similar to white-collar workers in political views and life style, and having assimilated into a middle class way of life.

The *embourgeoisement* thesis also points to some changes in the objective conditions of work that have "bourgeoisified" traditional working class occupations. Profit sharing, self-employment, and commissions as sources of income to workers have increased the number of *petit bourgeois* positions in the occupational structure, thereby impeding the development of worker consciousness and class formation (Russell, 1983).

Critics of the *embourgeoisement* thesis have questioned the view of declining differences between blue- and white-collar workers. Goldthorpe *et al.* (1968) report findings from a study of affluent manual workers that show little change in political attachments of workers whose standard of living has become middle class. Research by Rinehart (1971) and DeFranzo (1973) also concludes that there are substantial differences between manual and nonmanual workers, and that even the most skilled and affluent manual workers do not have attitudes and behaviors similar to white-collar workers. The weight of the research evidence indicates that both working class affluence and the *embourgeoisement* thesis have been exaggerated, and that blue-collar workers still have the potential to react to their social and economic situation with a sense of class-based antagonism.[2]

---

[2]This is so because the root "cause" of class conflict lies in the fact that capitalists own and/or control the means of production and workers sell their labor power, the outcome of which is capital's appropriation of surplus value.

Efforts to identify the sources of worker consciousness have focused on structural factors associated with the work situation (e.g., autonomy, skill level, labor market segments) and nonwork factors, such as social background and political socialization (Tanner and Cockerill, 1986). In this chapter we emphasize the role of the work situation in shaping worker consciousness and the special circumstances that a plant closing creates for the development of greater worker consciousness and militancy.

Plant Closing and Worker Consciousness

As discussed in Chapter 1, the last decade has seen an acceleration in the pace of change in American industry. The shift of basic industries from the United States to lower wage markets outside of the country has resulted in an increase in plant closings and relocations, causing abrupt and unexpected unemployment for tens of thousands of workers (Bluestone and Harrison, 1982). Reductions in industrial production, and reinvestment in other economic sectors, has also resulted in hundreds of thousands of layoffs. The Bureau of National Affairs (1983) estimates that in 1982 more than 1.2 million workers were placed on either temporary or permanent layoff. Approximately 215,000 workers lost their jobs as a result of some 600 incidents of permanent plant shutdown.

Research on plant closings in the late 1950s and early 1960s indicates that workers who experience the economic shock of unemployment often respond in ways that are relevant to the understanding of worker consciousness. A notable example of such research is Aiken *et al.*'s (1968) study of auto workers who were displaced by the closing of Packard Motor Car Company in Detroit in 1956. They were concerned with determining the relative influence of workers' economic deprivation, employment status, age, education, and skill level upon their social integration into society. Social integration was estimated by such measures as alienation, life satisfaction, social participation, and political extremism. Their findings indicate that economic deprivation has the strongest association with alienation, life satisfaction, social participation, as well as attitudes favoring government intervention to keep the plant open, providing aid to displaced workers, and government takeover of the plant. Especially significant is the fact that economic deprivation was more strongly associated with social integration than was employment status (measured as continuously unemployed, reemployed but presently unemployed, and presently employed).

Similar findings were obtained by Palen (1969) who studied workers displaced by the closing of the Studebaker plant in South Bend, Indiana in 1963. Support for radical action by government to intervene and take control of the plant was strongly associated with workers' degree of economic hardship, but not with employment status, occupation, age, race, or income. Once again, it is not employment status but economic hardship/distress that produces a radical response among displaced workers.

In contrast to general unemployment (i.e., that which is due to periodic demand-related cutbacks in production), plant closings eliminate a number of the barriers to group consciousness. First is the fact that the dislocated workers are more likely to know each other and to share information about their situation. Since an entire plant has closed, displaced workers will be less likely to attribute job loss to their individual inadequacies as workers and will look for causes elsewhere. If the plant that closes is unionized, there is likely to be active labor-management negotiations about the closing, creating the possibility of union mobilization of worker discontent. And, in some cases, a plant may have a work force that is more homogeneous racially, ethnically, and by skill level than a national sample of unemployed workers.

In short, the conditions surrounding a plant closing are more conducive to development of worker consciousness than would be found among unemployed workers generally. Indirect evidence for this hypothesis can be found in the contrasting findings of two studies of the relationship between unemployment and class consciousness. One piece of research by Leggett (1964), which was conducted on a sample of employed and unemployed workers in Detroit, revealed substantial differences in class consciousness. In contrast, a study by Schlozman and Verba (1979), which was based on a national sample of workers, reported almost no difference in class consciousness between employed and unemployed workers.

While the research by Leggett does not involve a plant closing, it does involve a single geographic location. This may provide workers with a common point of reference when answering questions about their economic problems and their responses to such problems. It also underscores the importance of focusing on historically specific situations when trying to assess worker consciousness. Using national samples of workers to assess worker or class consciousness seems to assume that such collective beliefs emerge spontaneously rather than in a context of mutual education among workers, and between them and political organizations that can mobilize and direct their discontent.

Theoretical Framework

Our purpose is to assess the extent of development of worker consciousness, which is a heightened sense of awareness of the interests that workers have in common and an understanding of the actions that can serve their interests. The concept of worker consciousness, as applied to the experience of displaced workers, is viewed as having three components: (1) an awareness of class inequalities; (2) an awareness of conflicting interests of workers and management; and (3) readiness to support political actions that will advance workers' interests.

Our approach suggests that it is profitable to study worker consciousness in historically specific situations, even though the structural conditions of the larger society are not necessarily favorable to the formation of class-wide political action. The conceptualization of worker consciousness as containing several stages of development or dimensions follows the approach to class consciousness suggested by Morris and Murphy (1966), Leggett (1964), Mann (1973), Buttel and Flinn (1979), and Zingraff and Schulman (1984). It permits us to think in terms of the extent of worker consciousness and it encourages theoretical consideration of the conditions that are favorable or inimical to its development.

Figure 7.1 presents the theoretical model of the variables that are hypothesized to influence worker consciousness (see also Table 7.1 for a description of how each variable is measured). The variables are ordered in a way that describes the process by which worker consciousness develops. We begin with age and gender of the displaced workers. Age is expected to vary inversely with worker consciousness. Younger workers should have more negative and militant responses to their unemployment because of disillusionment with mobility myths and greater economic insecurity (Buttel and Flinn, 1979). Older workers with grown children and somewhat better financial situations will have more conservative responses to the closing, including using the situation to accept an early retirement.

Gender is another characteristic of the displaced workers that can have an effect on worker consciousness. One view of women's reactions in comparison with men is that they might be less committed to their jobs or may be a second family wage earner and therefore less critical or militant with regard to the closing. Another view, however, is that women are as involved with work as men and are subject to greater economic insecurity than men, thereby making them potentially more critical and militant. Our expectation, based on our own

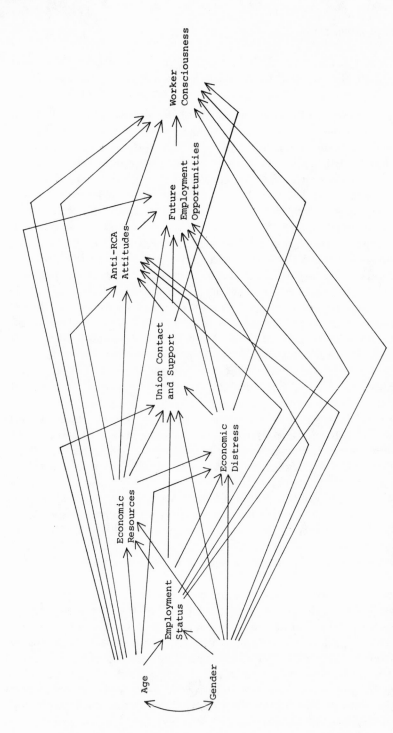

Figure 7.1. Theoretical model of development of worker consciousness.

findings in Chapter 6 and other research (Schulman *et al.*, 1985) is that gender will not be related to worker consciousness, because women do not differ significantly from men in their work commitments and their reactions to unemployment.

We next hypothesize that age and gender will be related to employment status. As reported in Chapter 4, older workers and women are more likely than younger workers and men to be continuously unemployed following the plant closing. Current employment status of displaced RCA workers, in turn, should be related to economic insecurity, a condition that is hypothesized to be most strongly associated with worker consciousness.

Economic insecurity can exist for both employed and unemployed workers. Those employed in low-paying jobs must live with limited economic resources, which can generate high levels of individual discontent (Schlozman and Verba, 1979). Low-status jobs also have high insecurity, which adds the problem of an unpredictable future that prevents planning and a sense of control over one's life. When those in low-paying, insecure jobs are also racial or ethnic minorities, there is the added burden of institutionalized discrimination which can exacerbate feelings of discontent and strain (Zingraff and Schulman, 1984).

Table 7.1. Measurement of Variables Used in Theoretical Model

1. **Age:** 1983 minus year of birth
2. **Gender:** male = 1, female = 2
3. **Employment status:** unemployed = 1, employed part-time = 2, employed full time = 3
4. **Economic resources:** the total number of sources of income available to respondent including respondent's salary, spouse's salary, unemployment compensation of respondent, unemployment compensation of spouse, severance pay, savings.
5. **Economic distress:** summary score of responses to six questions about whether they can afford clothing, adequate food, furniture or household equipment in need of replacement, leisure activities, a suitable home, and a car; and two questions about difficulty in paying bills. The higher the summary score the more economic distress.
6. **Union contact and support:** summary of six items on frequency of attendance at union local meetings, request for assistance from Workers' Aid Council, and degree of satisfaction with union efforts in areas of wages, health benefits, retirement benefits, and grievances. The higher the summary score the more contact with and support from the union.

(*continued*)

Table 7.1. *(Continued)*

7. **Anti-RCA attitudes:** degree of agreement with two items stating that the already profitable RCA plant closed in order to (a) increase profits and (b) break the union.

8. **Future employment opportunities:** summary score of five items reflecting respondent's view of employment in the future ("There is a good job waiting for me if I just look harder to find it," "No matter what I do it will be near impossible to find a job in the months ahead," "Finding a job is a matter of luck," "When the economy picks up I will find a job easily," "I will soon be able to get a job even if the economy doesn't pick up.") The higher the summary score the more optimistic about future employment.

8. **Worker consciousness:** summary score of items reflecting:
   a. Awareness of inequality: "Do you think that the child of a factory worker has about the same chance to get ahead as the child of a business executive, has a somewhat less chance to get ahead, or much less chance to get ahead?"
   b. Conflicting interests of management and workers: "Do you think that the interests of management and workers are basically opposed, interests basically the same, or mixed?"
   c. Egalitarian change: sum of responses to "The government should end unemployment by hiring everybody who is without a job," "The government should see that every family has enough money to have a decent standard of living," "The government should tax the rich heavily in order to redistribute wealth."
   The higher the summary score the greater worker consciousness.

The more extreme form of economic insecurity is job loss. Unemployment often results in immediate economic deprivation, long-term disruption of individual and family plans, interpersonal tensions with family and friends, and personal threats to one's self-esteem (Cohn, 1978). Joblessness results in the highest degree of subjective strain and discontent that can be mobilized into beliefs and actions expressive of worker consciousness. For example, Leggett (1964) found that the unemployed were more militant and class conscious than employed blue-collar workers in Detroit.

As reported in the present study (Chapter 4), displaced workers have experienced job insecurity and economic hardship associated with job loss. Although all respondents have been displaced by a plant closing, they have experienced different degrees of economic hardship depending upon alternative sources of money and whether or not they have been reemployed. We neither treat all displaced workers as experiencing the same degree of hardship and insecurity, nor expect them to subjectively react to that hardship in the same way. Both objective and subjective levels of hardship are examined for their correspondence and their effects. We expect that both objective and perceived economic hardship will be directly related to worker consciousness.

In Figure 7.1 there are arrows from employment status to economic resources and economic distress. These indicate that we hypothesize that the continuously unemployed will report having fewer economic resources and greater economic distress. We also hypothesize that the amount of economic resources a displaced worker has will be inversely related to the degree of economic distress he/she reports.

Displaced workers who are continuously unemployed and who have fewer economic resources and experience higher levels of economic distress are expected to have greater contact with their union after the plant closing. Going to the union hall after the plant closing probably reflects an established pattern of greater involvement with the union as well as the hope that continued contact might provide leads on new jobs or information about the endless rumors that the plant was going to reopen under a new owner.

Whatever the motivation of displaced workers to maintain contact with other workers through the union, such contact provides an opportunity to discuss common problems and concerns. The union hall also provides an organized setting for discussing the closing and its consequences, thereby increasing the chances that discontent can be mobilized into worker consciousness and group action. It was the union that organized meetings in the union hall with elected officials and community leaders to discuss the problems of displaced RCA workers. It was the active union members who formed the Workers Aid Council to assist workers with their personal problems, unemployment checks, and finding a new job. And it was the union that pressured the Employment Security Division to provide space in the union hall so that workers would not have to travel to another town to sign for unemployment compensation.

Thus, we hypothesize that workers who have greater contact and solidarity with the union will exhibit greater worker consciousness. In addition, we expect greater contact to influence workers' ideas about why the RCA plant closed and about their opportunities for future employment.

We have already noted (Chapter 6) that displaced workers express a variety of opinions about why the RCA plant closed and hold different beliefs about their chances for reemployment. Some displaced workers are very critical of the closing decision, viewing the corporation as eager to expand profits or to break the power of unions. On the other hand, some view the corporation as being involved in a competitive struggle with foreign business and having little alternative but to close down. The experience of the closing left some workers with the feeling that their situation was unusual, in that the national economy was healthy and their chances for reemployment were good. On the other hand, others were very pessimistic about the economy as a whole and their own chances for finding another good job. We expect workers who are more critical of the RCA corporation for closing the plant to have greater worker consciousness. We also expect greater consciousness among workers who are pessimistic about future employment opportunities.

To summarize, we expect worker consciousness following a plant closing to be greatest when there is economic hardship, greater union involvement and solidarity, and a perception of corporate actions and the economy that puts all workers at great economic risk. These conditions reflect the theoretical proposition that worker consciousness develops when there is (1) economic deprivation, (2) an opportunity for workers to communicate with each other about their shared problem, and (3) a perception of the connections between the causes and consequences of their "class situation."

Development of Worker Consciousness

Before examining data relevant to the theoretical model presented in Figure 7.1 we note again the fact that our data on displaced workers were obtained after the plant closed. Thus, we have no indication of how much, if at all, the experience of unemployment may have influenced workers' beliefs and behavior. In fact, it is possible (but not likely) that the displaced workers were more militant and radical before the plant closed and that the experience of the closing resulted in greater political passivity. To approach this question we compare responses of displaced workers with those of the workers in a manufacturing plant in the same community.

Table 7.2 contains the distribution of responses to the five questions that were used to estimate worker consciousness for both displaced RCA workers and continuously employed workers in Monticello. For all of the items, displaced workers reveal a higher degree of worker consciousness than employed workers. The observed differences are

Table 7.2. Responses to Worker Consciousness Questions

	Displaced Workers (%)	Continuously Employed Workers (%)
1. Awareness of inequality: "Do you think that the child of a factory worker has about the same chance to get ahead as the child of a business executive?" (percentage saying "much less")	34	17**
2. Conflicting interests: "Do you think that the interests of management and workers are basically opposed?" (percentage agreeing)	15	7
3. Egalitarian change: "Government should hire people without jobs" (percentage agreeing)	42	14**
"Government should see that every family has enough money: (percentage agreeing)	67	26***
"Government should tax the rich heavily and redistribute wealth: (percentage agreeing)	58	52

***$p \leq .001$
**$p \leq .02$

statistically significant for "awareness of inequality" and for two of the measures of "egalitarian change," but not for "worker-management conflict." Such findings are contrary to Schlozman and Verba's (1979) findings of no difference in class consciousness between employed and unemployed workers, and thus provide tentative support for our view that workers who are unemployed because of a plant closing may be different from unemployed workers in general.

We now return to the basic theoretical model and the data used to estimate the level of empirical support for it. The zero-order correlations of all the variables contained in the model are provided in Table 7.3. Figure 7.1 presents the theoretical model and Figure 7.2 describes all of the significant path coefficients in the model. Table 7.4 presents the standard regression coefficients and standard errors for each of the hypothesized links between variables of the fully identified model.

Table 7.3. Zero-Order Correlations

	1	2	3	4	5	6	7	8	9
1. Age	—								
2. Gender	–.10	—							
3. Employment status	–.30	–.14	—						
4. Economic resources	.09	–.06	.11	—					
5. Economic distress	–.10	–.02	–.06	–.18	—				
6. Union contact/support	.06	–.06	.01	.07	.14	—			
7. Anti-RCA attitudes	–.01	–.01	.07	.14	.00	.12	—		
8. Future employment opportunities	–.16	.10	.19	.19	–.20	.04	.03	—	
9. Worker consciousness	–.07	–.04	–.04	–.13	.32	.02	–.02	–.25	—

138

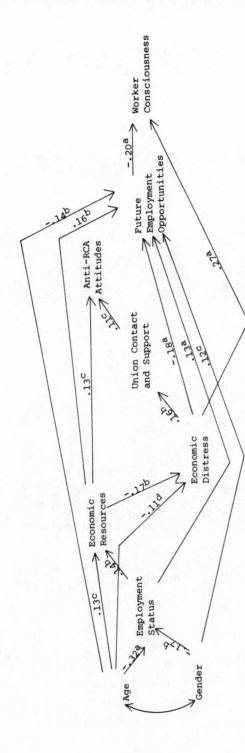

Figure 7.2. Significant path coefficients.

Table 7.4. Regression Coefficients for the Path Model

Dependent Variable	Independent Variable	Standardized Regression Coefficient	Regression Coefficient	Standard Error
Worker consciousness $R^2 = .15$	Age	−.075	−.012	.009
	Gender	−.028	−.092	.176
	Employment status	−.006	−.015	.121
	Economic resources	−.040	−.058	.079
	Economic distress	.268[a]	.190	.039
	Union contact/support	.003	.002	.038
	Anti-RCA attitudes	−.005	−.005	.055
	Future employment opportunities	−.197[a]	−.130	.037
Future employment opportunities $R^2 = .13$	Age	−.145[b]	−.034	.014
	Gender	.119[c]	.587	.268
	Employment status	.134[c]	.426	.184
	Economic resources	.157[b]	.341	.120
	Economic distress	−.183[a]	−.196	.059
	Union contact/support	.070	.075	.058
	Anti-RCA attitudes	−.005	−.008	.083
Anti-RCA attitudes $R^2 = .04$	Age	−.004	−.001	.009
	Gender	.011	.035	.182
	Employment status	.057	.116	.125
	Economic resources	.126[c]	.177	.081
	Economic distress	.013	.009	.040
	Union contact/support	.114[c]	.079	.039

Union contact/support				
$R^2 = .03$	Age	$.071$	$.016$	$.013$
	Gender	$-.038$	$-.174$	$.263$
	Employment status	$.029$	$.087$	$.180$
	Economic resources	$.085$	$.173$	$.117$
	Economic distress	$.161^a$	$.161$	$.058$
Economic distress				
$R^2 = .05$	Age	$-.111^d$	$-.024$	$.013$
	Gender	$-.051$	$-.235$	$.259$
	Employment status	$-.086$	$-.255$	$.177$
	Economic resources	$-.169^b$	$-.340$	$.114$
Economic resources				
$R^2 = .03$	Age	$.132^c$	$.014$	$.006$
	Gender	$-.032$	$-.074$	$.129$
	Employment status	$.144^b$	$.212$	$.087$
Employment status				
$R^2 = .12$	Age	$-.320^a$	$-.023$	$.004$
	Gender	$-.170^b$	$-.262$	$.082$

[a] $= .001$
[b] $= .01$
[c] $= .05$
[d] $= .10$

141

Economic distress and perceptions of future employment opportunities have the greatest effects upon worker consciousness (Table 7.4: beta = .268, $p \leq .001$ and beta = $-.197$, $p \leq .001$). As hypothesized, displaced workers who report greater economic distress and who have pessimistic feelings about their chances for future employment have higher worker consciousness. Contrary to our expectations, worker attitudes toward RCA and contact with the local labor union do not have effects on worker consciousness.

Worker perceptions of future employment opportunities are significantly influenced by each of the preceding variables, with the exception of attitudes toward RCA and union contact. Optimistic views of future employment prospects are more likely to be expressed by younger workers, women, the reemployed, those with more economic resources, and those who report less economic distress.

The displaced workers who report negative attitudes toward RCA for closing the plant are those with more economic resources and those with more union contact and solidarity. The latter finding is as we hypothesized, but the former is not. Workers with greater economic resources may be more negative toward RCA because they had more to lose by closing. Those with more years of experience at RCA may have the most resources and also the strongest expectations that the plant would continue to operate.

Greater union contact and support is significantly related to economic distress. Workers reporting greater distress have more contact with and more positive attitudes toward the union. This is probably due to the fact that those with the most financial difficulties sought out union officials for help with unemployment-welfare benefits or information about new job opportunities.

Workers reporting greater economic distress are more likely to be younger, to be unemployed, and to have fewer economic resources. Such findings are as expected. Also expected is the finding that older workers and those who are reemployed report having more economic resources. Finally, older workers and women are less likely to be employed 8 months after the RCA plant closed.

The significant path coefficients for the theoretical model are presented in Figure 7.2. This figure provides a summary picture of the direct and indirect links among variables hypothesized to be related to worker consciousness. Economic distress and perceived future employment opportunities have the largest significant direct effects on worker consciousness. These two variables also serve as indirect links to worker consciousness.

There are five indirect effects on worker consciousness through be-

liefs about future employment opportunities. As predicted, older workers perceived fewer employment opportunities, thereby increasing their
worker consciousness. Workers with fewer economic resources and more
economic distress perceived fewer employment opportunities, result-
ing in increased worker consciousness. Reemployed workers and women
have more optimistic views of future employment opportunities, re-
sulting in reduced worker consciousness.

As hypothesized, economic distress leads to greater involvement with
the local union which, in turn, is related to anti-RCA attitudes. However, contrary to expectations, these factors do not directly or indirectly
increase worker consciousness.

Perceived economic distress is greater among younger workers and
those with fewer economic resources. The influence of age on worker
consciousness is mediated by economic resources, economic distress,
and perceptions of future employment opportunities.

The general pattern of relationships indicated by the significant path
coefficients suggests the following process. The most vulnerable displaced workers are those who remain unemployed longer. As a result
of being unemployed longer they have fewer economic resources, greater
perceived distress, and are more pessimistic about their future chances
for employment. Each of these factors, in turn, increases displaced
workers' awareness of inequality, their perception of management-
worker interests as being opposed, and their support for egalitarian
change.

The main hypotheses about the process by which workers develop
greater consciousness that are not supported concern involvement with
the union and anti-RCA attitudes. Workers with the greatest distress
did have greater contact with the union and this, in turn, increased the
expression of negative attitudes toward RCA for closing the plant.
However, union contact and a critical stance toward RCA did not
translate into pessimistic views of future employment opportunities or
increased worker consciousness.

Conclusions

We began this chapter with the general view that the growing number of plant closings presents a special and extreme case for understanding the negative impact of unemployment (for a similar view see
Kinichi, 1985). More specifically, we suggested that workers displaced
by a plant closing present an opportunity for the study of worker con-

sciousness that is not present in studies of unemployed workers in different locations and from different firms. Workers displaced by a plant closing would have a greater opportunity to meet and discuss their common problems, both before and after the closing. Such opportunities for interaction and solidarity could result in greater awareness of worker interests and agreement about actions that could advance them.

The theoretical model used to understand the process of development of worker consciousness emphasized the economic deprivation of displaced workers as the basic source of generalized discontent. Economic deprivation is based on limited resources and the continued vulnerability associated with long-term unemployment. A second stage in the process emphasized the opportunity to channel generalized discontent into specific beliefs about why the RCA plant closed and a recognition that the problem is not temporary but the beginning of chronic unemployment (i.e., structural unemployment). Thus, those who experience the most economic deprivation, and who have the opportunity to collectively discuss their problems, will develop the greatest worker consciousness.

The data used to test this theoretical model generally support the hypothesis that discontent based in economic deprivation and insecurity can be mobilized into worker consciousness. There is also some support for the hypothesized role of workers' perceptions of future employment as a link in the development of worker consciousness. However, involvement with the union and beliefs about why RCA closed did not serve as a mediating link to worker consciousness. One speculation to explain this contrary finding is that the terms of the union's closing agreement was a divisive issue among workers, especially with respect to early retirement and severance pay. This may have restricted the unions' role in mobilizing discontent to those workers who were satisfied with the terms of the closing contract.

In conclusion, there is some support for our model linking the economic deprivation of displaced workers to worker consciousness. Our findings also reveal greater worker consciousness among those workers unemployed due to a plant closing than is found in studies using a general sample of unemployed workers. This may be due to the fact that workers displaced by a plant closing have a more visible target for their discontent and are therefore less likely to blame themselves or unknown forces for their problems. The collective nature of their problem increases communication and provides group legitimacy for many of their attitudes and beliefs. In addition, the specific geographic location of the closing also links displaced workers to a single local labor market, perhaps giving them more realistic perceptions of their opportunities for reemployment.

We expect the increase in plant closings to facilitate opportunities for the expression of greater militancy by displaced workers, especially if there are organized efforts to mobilize and channel discontent. This is most likely to occur if worker-based organizations serve as a place where workers can gather to discuss their problems and provide the opportunity for collective action.

8

IMPLICATIONS FOR RESEARCH AND PUBLIC POLICY

In Chapter 1 the analysis of the Monticello experience was placed within the context of a global process of capital mobility. Drawing upon the groundbreaking work of Bluestone and Harrison, the early chapters documented the flight of capital as a historical process of the 1970s and 1980s. This process had particularly profound negative consequences for the Midwest, and the state of Indiana. Because of the logic of capital flight, the pursuit of cheaper labor, and the drive to overcome declining profit margins, there was little possibility that the Monticello RCA workers could forestall the plant closing.

Given this broader background of capital mobility of which the Monticello, Indiana case is just one among thousands, *both* research and public policy debate on plant closings remain vital for social scientists and political activists. Consequently, the Monticello study raises three questions for consideration in our concluding discussions. First, given the findings reported in this book what should the future research agenda on plant closings include? Second, what relevance do the reported findings have to the debate on public policy concerning unemployment and plant closings? Third, given the fact that workers and communities are the victims of plant closings, what can labor and community coalitions do to ameliorate or reverse this historic process of capital flight? Each of these questions will be addressed in this conclusion.

Future Research on Plant Closings

The findings of the Monticello project encompass economic, health, social, psychological, and ideological impacts of the plant closing. Data indicated the negative consequences of the closing on social service agencies, local businesses, and economic and political elites' expectations about the future. Of great economic consequence also was the large percentage of workers who were still unemployed after 8 months, and, among those with new jobs, had much lowered wage levels. In terms of family financial matters, workers reported deep cuts in purchases and increases in home production. According to the data, women were less likely to be rehired than men and if reemployed at lower wages than men.

Effects on their physical and mental health were also reported by workers. Increases in several symptoms of distress were noted as well as increases in drinking and smoking. RCA workers expressed greater depression and a lower sense of mastery over their lives than a group of continuously employed workers. RCA workers were also more pessimistic about their future than the other group of workers. For all types of impacts, women were affected as adversely as men. On the other hand, the situation of older workers was no worse than that of younger workers, 8 months after the closing. Reemployment did not help workers to overcome the effects of the closing. Finally, low levels of mastery, cutbacks in family expenses, and low social support were all related to depression among the displaced workers.

Our research findings also demonstrate the impact of the closing on the displaced workers' beliefs and political ideology. RCA workers exhibited a high degree of alienation from their society, as indicated by their reactions to local and national social institutions. When compared to a group of employed workers, the displaced workers were more likely to express a lack of confidence in their leaders and institutions. Expressions of alienation in the attitudes and beliefs of displaced workers did not differ markedly for workers of different age, gender, or employment status. This indicates that (1) both women and men have similar political responses to their unemployment, and (2) even when displaced workers become reemployed they continue to be alienated.

The experience of the plant closing led some workers to develop higher levels of worker consciousness, as reflected in their identification with common political and economic interests of workers. Displaced workers exhibited greater worker consciousness than was found among employed workers in the same community, indicating that the experience of the plant closing influenced their thinking about political and economic issues. The source of worker consciousness among displaced workers was traced to their level of economic deprivation and their pessimism about their future job opportunities. In short, those workers who experienced great economic distress and who saw little hope for a better future were the most militant in their search for solutions to their problems.

These findings on alienation and worker consciousness also allow us to speculate that workers displaced by plant closings have different political reactions than individuals unemployed through layoffs. Plant closing experiences may make it clear to workers that broader economic and political forces, rather than their own idiosyncratic flaws, are responsible for their unemployment.

The findings suggest that the transformations of the U.S. economy and their impacts on communities and workers are significant. Consequently, there is a need to extend the research agenda to further our knowledge of the plant closing phenomena.

First, many of the findings reported above were discerned from modest statistical relationships. Other tendencies noted were not reflected in statistically significant correlations. Part of the problem from a research standpoint was the time frame utilized in this study. Workers were queried 8 months after the closing and aggregate community impacts were based upon figures just 1 year after the closing. As various persons interviewed at the time indicated, the worst impacts of the closing were still to be experienced: unemployment benefits and severance pay would end; savings would dwindle; former RCA employees would leave the community; demands on social services would rise. Therefore, future plant closing research designs should encompass a longer time frame and/or a follow-up procedure. The theoretical literature and the findings reported above would suggest that the impacts of a closing on a community and its workers would be even more devastating after 1, 2, or 5 years then just 8 months (Craypo and Davisson, 1983).

Also, future research on plant closings should be more comparative in perspective. For a variety of theoretical reasons, one might expect variations of impacts on workers and communities in settings with different worker–management relationships and different levels of worker organization. First, plant closing researchers should be interested to see whether impacts vary within large vs. small plants in big cities or small towns. It may be that impacts, particularly at the level of worker consciousness, will be greater in larger firms in small towns because of the disproportionately large role the plant has on the local economy.

However, the ripple effects on political consciousness could be greater in larger cities if major plants are closing or threatening to close. As to physical and psychological effects, the larger community setting may be better able to reemploy and support unemployed workers than smaller communities.

A further variation involves the kind of plant experiencing the closing. Some plants manufacture commodities that are produced by numerous other plants such that job relocation is a possibility. Others represent relatively unusual product lines in which only a few plants satisfy the need for the industry. This consideration relates to the skill level of the workers required in the plant, the level of automation of the plant, and the amount of overseas production of the product.

Also, corporations vary as to the state of worker–management relations. This is nowhere better illustrated than in a plant closing situation. Many corporations give workers virtually no notice of the closing (in some cases no notice), others give 6 months to 1 year and provide training for new jobs or for new job-searching skills. Some workers negotiate closing agreements that provide short-term support after the closing and other workers receive nothing. These variations may affect the physical and psychological state and consciousness of workers. Good worker–management relations may reduce somewhat the most deleterious effects of the closing compared with companies with poor worker–management relations.

Further, the impacts of the closing may vary in union vs. non-union plants and in plants where the union is a significant force among the workers compared with settings where union organization and influence is weak. In the Monticello case, the union was a central force in the plant and the community and the Workers Aid Council was particularly important in its efforts to aid displaced workers. Finally, researchers may want to assess the impacts of closings in a community on employed workers: on heightened work pressures, speed-ups, and fears of job loss. Plant closings may significantly affect others than those displaced.

The general theme of plant closing research remains the same: that is, to discover what happens to workers and their communities after a plant closing. How does the closing affect income, jobs, physical health, psychic well-being, and political consciousness. Moving beyond the Monticello project, these questions can be better addressed by engaging in the kinds of longitudinal and comparative research efforts suggested.

Relevance of Findings to Public Policy

The evidence presented throughout this volume is that the U.S. economy is experiencing enormous changes due to capital flight and that the ramifications for communities and workers has been great. Consequently, because of the individual and social costs of plant closings, there is a need for a much expanded policy response to this veritable disease at the local, state, and national levels.

However, current national policy does not acknowledge the link between fiscal and monetary policies and unemployment. For example, politicians and economists are reluctant to admit that increased unemployment has often been used in the past as a policy tool for "cooling off" an economy faced with high inflation. Similarly, unemployment and plant closings are seen as normal and unavoidable costs of a growing and changing economy in a "free market." It is also argued that workers need to retrain to perform in a modern economy and that plants or industries that face decline do so because of shifting markets, new competitors, inefficient operations, and old facilities. Thus the U.S. economy must change to maintain its prominent world position. From this perspective, plant closings and the displacement of workers presage a growing and changing economy that is responsive to the challenges of the 1980s and 1990s. It is simply in the very nature of economic life that some firms fail and others succeed.

In the context of an economy experiencing "creative destruction," opponents of plant closing policies argue, the economic stress of unemployment are met by unemployment insurance, severance pay, and various welfare "safety nets." The unemployment experience of the late 1980s, it is argued, is different from that of the 1930s when there were no public policies providing temporary support to needy workers.

However, studies suggest that current social programs do not help a majority of those experiencing unemployment. Margolis and Farran (1984) report that unemployment assistance is available to less than one-half of the unemployed, and that the amount and duration of benefits for those who are eligible rarely exceeds 50% of a worker's average weekly wage. They also report the results of a Department of Labor survey which indicates that only a little more than one-third of all workers in large unionized companies with more than 1000 workers have severance pay provisions in their contracts.

Current policy also fails to recognize that when unemployment occurs during a recession, or a large plant closes in a small community, there is also a decline in the availability of community resources to assist displaced workers. Ferman's (1984) analysis of the plight of the unemployed in Michigan during the 1980–1981 recession points to two things that occur as unemployment rises. First, there are reductions in state and federal funds for human services as revenues decline. Second, there is increased competition for shrinking resources among advocates for the unemployed, the aged, the poor, business and the community, and for the infrastructure of roads and schools.

The closest that current policy comes to assisting the structurally unemployed worker is through the Trade Adjustment Act (TAA) and Title III of the Job Training and Partnership Act (JTPA). The former provides some service and retraining benefits to workers whose unemployment is due to international competition, and the latter provides retraining for workers whose jobs have been eliminated. Neither act provides for more than a tiny minority of needy workers and funds since these programs have been cut in recent years. In sum, many economists and policymakers argue that the U.S. economy is experiencing a major transformation; that out of the tragedy of high unemployment and plant closings will come a newly revitalized pattern of economic growth that will benefit American workers in the future. Others, like Bluestone and Harrison (1982), state that the processes of capital flight and deindustrialization of the U.S. have caused a worsening of the living conditions of workers as they shift from high-paying manufacturing jobs to low-paying service jobs.

To counter the latter possible future, many political economists and labor activists have been proposing various policy options to save communities, jobs, and incomes from the devastating effects of capital flight and plant closings. A common proposal made by scholars and activists is plant closing legislation. The most significant feature of plant closing legislation is that it places employment and the human and social costs of unemployment at the center of economic decision-making. While there are many differences in federal and state proposals for such legislation, a bill proposed in the Indiana State Legislature is illustrative. It included prior notification of intention to close of at least 6 months; a public hearing to determine whether the closing is necessary; severance pay for workers; 1 year of continuous health coverage for workers following a shutdown; job transfer privileges; funds for worker retraining, and a lump-sum payment to the community to ease the transition to declining public resources.

The need for the provisions usually contained in plant closing legislation is suggested by the absence of employee protection in many union contracts. Mick's (1975) examination of 1823 contracts in bargaining units with at least 1000 employees finds mention of the following provisions in relation to plant closings: interplant transfers (32.1%); severance pay (29.6%); relocation allowance (11.1%); transfer of seniority rights (9.9%); income maintenance (5.1%); advance notice of a closing (3.7%); and notification to and participation of unions in plant closing decisions (3.3%). Mick estimated that only about 25% of unionized workers (who constitute less than 20% of the work force) are covered by plant closing provisions in their contracts.

The rationale for plant closing legislation is threefold. First, the existence of such legislation will slow down capital flight because it will make disinvestment less attractive to corporate decision-makers. Second, even if a closing occurs, the obligation of the corporation to workers and their communities will help reduce the human and social costs of the closing. Third, given the costs of a closing to the firm as well as the community, it would be less expensive to modernize an old facility than to build a totally new facility in another location in the U.S. or overseas.

While critics of plant closing legislation argue that such policies would stifle economic growth and the need for corporate freedom, proponents of the legislation point to the more rigorous legislative limitations on corporate action in virtually every other industrial capitalist country, with little indication that such constraints have damaged economic development. For example, a delegation representing the United Auto Workers, the United Steelworkers of America, and the International Association of Machinists visited Sweden, West Germany, and England in 1978 to study economic policies on corporate flight. They wrote:

> In all three countries, corporations are legally obligated to give advance notice (to) workers, unions, and the employment service before closing a plant or dismissing workers for economic reasons. Before initiating layoffs, moreover, a company must first negotiate the matter with its employees union or the plants' works joint labor-management council. . . . The time gained gives affected workers and potential new employees the chance to arrange for alternative employment . . . advance notice triggers into action labor market boards at the national, regional, local (and in some cases, workplace) levels (in Bluestone and Harrison 1982, p. 237).

Of the three countries mentioned, Sweden has the most advanced policies. All employers are required to list their vacancies and such lists are provided to workers who are being displaced by unemployment. The Swedish government supports public enterprises to create new jobs for the jobless. Also the government provides grants and loans for new private sector business startups. In West Germany, companies planning a closing must give reasons to local works councils, including the availability of financial books, to assess the impact the closing would have on the region. In France, laws require management/worker committee consultations. The company projecting a closing must submit data and have layoff proposals certified as to their necessity. Workers must receive advance notice of a closing and 1-month's wages as severance pay. A company that has engaged in layoffs cannot hire new workers without government approval. Rothstein (1986) claims that the French plant closing laws have led to "soft layoffs" rather than precipitous plant closings. "Soft layoffs" include planned hiring freezes, attractive severance packages to encourage workers to leave their jobs, lowered retirement ages, and other less painful strategies to reduce the number of employees.

A comparison of the European case with that of the United States shows the paucity of policy in support of workers in the latter. Only two states have any such legislation. Maine requires 60-day advance notice to workers of an impending closing and severance pay for factories with more than 100 workers. Wisconsin has legislation suggesting a voluntary 60-day notice of a planned closing. A few cities, such as Pittsburgh, Philadelphia, and Vacaville, California passed local laws requiring notice. Vacaville also created an ordinance requiring companies relocating to town to meet standards for displaced workers in their former location before receiving any redevelopment assistance. Plant closing legislation has been introduced occasionally in over twenty states and legislators in Congress have proposed national legislation, to no avail. Consequently, despite much grassroots effort, plant closing legislation has not generated sufficient support from legislative bodies.

There is also much opposition to the creation of a comprehensive industrial policy based upon political input from government, the corporate sector, and organized labor. Various proposals for industrial policy emphasize governmental financing to maintain the U.S. manufacturing sector, government stimuli for regional development in hard hit areas like the Midwest, and trade policies that protect American manufacturing.

Further, some critics of U.S. economic policy argue for comprehensive programs of social welfare to mute the effects of the changing economy and to aid the non-unionized, low-wage, and nonorganized laboring sectors of society. These proposals include guarantees of severance pay and unemployment compensation commensurate with satisfactory living standards. Also expanded social welfare legislation would involve improved income supports, national health insurance, child care, aid to education, and expanded delivery of human services at the community level. Such programs would also assist casualties of economic change whether or not they were unemployed or even in the labor force.

There is no question that responses to plant closings and unemployment should be supported in conjunction with expanded social welfare legislation in the context of an industrial policy derived from popular participation. The goal of these approaches to the grievous changes the U.S. economy is experiencing is to improve the quality of life of American citizens. Long ago Franklin Roosevelt spoke of the need for an Economic Bill of Rights that guaranteed a job to everyone who wanted one at a fair wage, adequate housing and education, accessible medical care, and equal opportunities for all citizens (Boyer and Morais, 1955).

The research reported in this book illustrates one case of uncontrolled economic change which has created long-term consequences for the workers involved and the larger community. A public policy committed to maintaining the viability of the local economy and the basic standard of living of the workers affected by the plant closing seems to be the most appropriate way to respond to the historic movement of capital on a worldwide basis.

Workers' Response to Plant Closings

Since the phenomenon of plant closings have become a permanent feature of economic life in the 1980s, workers and communities have begun to develop responses to the threat and actuality of specific closings and to organize around the issue of deindustrialization at large. Examining worker responses before, during, and after closing situations will give some sense of options available to those experiencing or anticipating plant closings.

First, workers have begun to look for early warning signs of a possible closing within their own factories. These signs include a company opening a new plant producing the same product, the factory facilities beginning to deteriorate, no replacements for outdated machinery, a reduction in the number of product lines manufactured in the plant, cut-backs on overtime, layoffs, movements of managers to other sites, and reductions in advertising of the product line.

If several signs indicate a prospective closing or if the company announces a future closing, workers have organized community-labor coalitions to forestall the closing or to improve the terms of the closing.

Several such coalitions around the country have mobilized to fight closings in their communities. For example, when the Nabisco Company announced it would be closing a plant in Pittsburgh the Save Nabisco Action Coalition (SNAC) was formed consisting of labor, religious, and other community people. The coalition discovered that Nabisco operations were profitable and therefore worked to forestall the closings. SNAC also learned that a number of the Nabisco Board of Directors were on the Board of Directors of a local bank and distributed postcards to be sent to the bank notifying it that accounts would be withdrawn. Further, the Bakers, Confectioners and Tobacco Union announced it would carry out a nationwide strike of all Nabisco plants. The combination of local financial pressures and support from the international union led Nabisco to revise its decision. The Nabisco Coalition then continued its work to secure a plant closing ordinance for the city of Pittsburgh (Haas, 1985).

Another victory was achieved in New Bedford, Massachusetts at the Morse Tool Company, owned by Gulf and Western. During contract negotiations, Gulf and Western threatened to close the company if the workers refused to accept concessions. The United Electrical Workers local (UE) got assistance from a research group that determined that Gulf and Western was acting in conformance with a national divestment strategy. UE publicized the results of the study and their modest wage demands at a luncheon of local religious and political leaders. Gulf and Western refused to accept the UE wage offer and a lengthy strike resulted. The union, in coalition with other concerned citizens, demanded that Gulf and Western invest more in Morse Tool or sell to another corporation that would. Both the New Bedford city council and the Massachusetts House of Representatives passed resolutions supporting the continued operation of Morse Tool. The public campaign led Gulf and Western to settle the wage dispute without concessions and keep the plant open. Two years later Gulf and Western announced its plans to sell Morse Tool. The city said it would use its power of eminent domain if a suitable buyer were not found. After further pressures on the company a buyer acceptable to the community and the UE local was found. In the aftermath of the struggles, the president of the local commented on the need for broad-based coalitions to forestall plant closings:

> Do everything possible. Rally the city or the town behind the workers. Without the support of the community forget it. Together we saved Morse for the city as well as for the workers. (Haas, 1985, p. 40)

Of course, many campaigns to defeat plant closings have failed (Lynd, 1982). The activities in the Mahoning Valley by an ecumenical coalition combining religious leaders and steel workers was unable to stop the closures of several steel plants in the Youngstown area. The ecumenical coalition's efforts to buy out closing steel mills floundered when the Carter Administration decided not to finance the buyout. However, other coalition efforts led to the organization of food banks, struggles for the extension of unemployment benefits, medical care, and an end to home foreclosures encompassing the Ohio and Pennsylvania Monongahela River Valley area.

Other movements to forestall plant closings have involved picketing, boycotting, the take over and running of grocery stores, and media campaigns. Lawrence Rothstein (1986) analyzed comparatively responses to two closings in quite varied contexts: the coalition to stop steel plant closings in Youngstown Ohio mentioned above and the efforts of workers in Longwy France to resist a closing in an area dominated by steel production. In the French case, multiple strategies were used by three trade union federations at *both* the local and national levels to resist the shutdown. Longwy workers immediately upon hearing of the closing announcement took the lead in a fightback struggle. They organized demonstrations, strikes, factory occupations, and even sabotage. They used media campaigns to mobilize local and national support by establishing their own radio station. Two of the three national union confederations prepared in advance of the closing a detailed proposal for renovating the whole steel industry. These plans suggested that the workers' organizations had sufficient expertise to be involved in the process of dialogue on national policy. The unions involved displayed electronic signs, had mass demonstrations in Longwy and Paris, occupied meeting rooms of the enterprise committee, blocked railroad tracks and highways, organized demonstrations of school children and women's groups, engineered work stoppages, and other activities. During the course of the struggle, the government increased benefits for displaced workers and announced bonuses for early retirement. In the end the unions and companies involved signed an agreement in July, 1979. These efforts did not keep the plants open but the agreement provided for the closing of several plants to occur without layoffs. Provisions of the agreement included early retirement, voluntary departure bonuses, job transfers, and postponements in some job reductions.

Rothstein claims that the French workers were able to receive significantly better closing terms than Youngstown workers because their strategies and levels of organization were much more militant. There was early and full involvement of national unions in Longwy, which was not found in the U.S. case. Workers were at the forefront of the struggle in France from the very beginning; in Youngstown, religious leaders and friends of labor were more active at the outset than workers themselves. Higher levels of community solidarity were achieved in Longwy than Youngstown. French workers had a higher degree of worker consciousness than U.S. workers and therefore saw plant closing issues as part of the struggle between capital and labor. More French workers viewed collective action as vital to self-protection from the closing than U.S. workers. Further, French workers were more likely to see layoffs as part of general features of the way a capitalist system works and the problems inherent to it than U.S. workers. Finally French workers saw their jobs as more integral to their quality of life than U.S. workers. Consequently, in terms of level of political action, coalition building, tactics, and political consciousness, Rothstein suggests, the French workers' response was substantially different from that of the U.S. workers.

Further, in terms of the general issue of worker response, actions in support of workers after a plant closes have been carried out. The Monticello example examined in this book indicates the importance of post-closing support group activities. The Workers Aid Council continued to advise displaced workers and to pressure sometimes recalcitrant or overworked social agencies. Also a labor research group supportive of the Monticello workers were able to acquire a job search training grant from the Comprehensive Education and Training Act to aid workers who had not had to look for a job in years. As suggested earlier, post-closing activities of this sort have been carried out by other coalitions, like the Ohio-Pennsylvania group, as well.

A difficult situation for workers following a plant closing is the fact that international union structures typically have been such that workers displaced by a closing no longer remain as members of their union. Displaced workers no longer pay union dues. Union halls no longer can be kept open and workers lose interest in their union ties. Recently the AFL-CIO has endorsed a policy of allowing "associate membership" in a union for those who are not part of a local. This has not yet adequately addressed the millions of workers who lost their jobs and the unions that worked on their behalf. If the plant closing experience politicizes workers as our data suggest, U.S. unions could be losing their most politically important members by not affording them continued status in the labor movement. This loss includes the leaders who emerged during the struggle to save jobs and to help displaced workers like members of the Workers Aid Council in Monticello.

The United Electrical Workers have tried to stimulate the formulation of Unemployment Councils, an idea with roots going back to the 1930s. By maintaining worker solidarity and collective action, displaced workers are better able to fight for their rights than as isolated individuals. However it occurs, it is clear from U.S. and other experiences, like the French case, workers must be organized to defend or enhance their rights.

Finally, coalitions of workers, religious leaders, and political activists have organized around struggles for plant closing legislation, new trade policies, and elements of a new industrial policy. These efforts are based on the assumption that to protect workers' rights there is a need to go beyond trade unionism, with its essential but more limited concentration on wages, benefits, and working conditions, to the building of a labor movement whose goal is to gain more state power so that the political process and the economic sector act more in conformance with the needs of the vast majority of the population.

There are sufficient indicators to suggest that the unbridled changes in the U.S. economy and their impacts as described in this volume could carry us into the 21st century with a work force that has been deskilled, marginalized, and reduced to poverty level incomes. To prevent this outcome, academic specialists, workers, religious, and political activists must begin to reshape their ideas about what constitutes a healthy economy and how to improve the quality of life for all and to communicate these ideas to the American people. Basic to this new thinking is the commitment to the rights of millions of working women and men to be treated with respect, to have a secure job, and to have an income that supports both the body and the spirit.

BIBLIOGRAPHY

Aiken, Michael, Ferman, Louis A., and Sheppard, Harold L.
   1968   *Economic failure, alienation and extremism.* Ann Arbor, MI:
          University of Michigan Press.
Alves, Wayne M. and Rossi, Peter H.
   1978   "Who should get what? Fairness judgements of the distri-
          bution of earnings." *American Journal of Sociology, 84:*541–
          64.
Aronson, Robert L. and McKersie, Robert B.
   1980   *Economic consequences of plant shutdowns in New York State.*
          Ithaca, NY: New York State School of Industrial and La-
          bor Relations, Cornell University.
Ashton, Patrick J. and Iadicola, Peter
   1986   "The differential impact of a plant closing on the re-em-
          ployment and income patterns of displaced blue- and
          white-collar employees." Paper presented at the annual
          meeting of the North Central Sociological Association, To-
          ledo, Ohio.
Blake, David H. and Walters, Robert S.
   1976   *The politics of global economic relations.* Englewood Cliffs, NJ:
          Prentice Hall.
Bluestone, Barry and Harrison, Bennett
   1982   *The Deindustrialization of America: Plant closings, commun-
          ity abandonment and the dismantling of basic industry.* Basic
          Books.

161

Blumstein, Michael
    1983   "Zenith regaining strength," *New York Times*, July 20, p. 25.

Boyer, Richard O. and Morris, Herbert M.
    1955   *Labor's untold story.* New York: United Electrical, Radio and Machine Workers of America (UE).

Brecher, Jeremy
    1979   "Roots of power: Employers and workers in the electrical products industry." *In* Andrew Zimbalist (Ed.), *Case studies on the labor process*, NY: Monthly Review, pp. 206–228.

Brenner, M. Harvey
    1973   *Mental illness and the economy.* Cambridge, MA: Harvard University Press.

Brown, Deborah, Pheasant, Jim, and Falck, Jeurene
    1983   *Stability and growth of economic sectors in Indiana counties. 1970–1980*, Station Bulletin No. 420, Department of Agricultural Economics, Agricultural Experiment Station, Purdue University.

Bryant, Rick
    1982a   "RCA puts off plant closing." *Lafayette Journal and Courier*, August 20, p. 1.
    1982b   "How far can a state go to keep industries?" *Lafayette Journal and Courier*, October 3, p. 1.

Bureau of National Affairs
    1983   *Layoffs, plant closings and concession bargaining.* Washington D.C.: Bureau of National Affairs, Inc.
    1984a   *BNA's Employee Relations Weekly.* 2, [8]: February 27, pp. 245–246.
    1984b   *BNA's Employee Relations Weekly*, 2, 9, March 5, p. 227.

Business Week
    1981   "RCA: Still another master," *2701*, August 17, pp. 80–86.

Buss, Terry F. and Redburn, F. Stevens
    1983   *Mass unemployment and community mental health.* Beverly Hills, CA: Sage.

Buttel, Frederick H. and Flinn, William L.
    1979   "Sources of working class consciousness." *Sociological Focus*, 12:37–52.

Catalano, Ralph and Dooley, David
    1977   "Economic predictors of depressed mood and stressful events in a metropolitan community." *Journal of Health and Social Behavior*, 18:292–307.
    1979   "Does economic change provoke or uncover behavioral

disorder? A preliminary test." *In* Louis A. Ferman and
Jeanne P. Gordus (Eds.), *Mental health and the economy.* Kalamazoo MI: W.E. Upjohn Institute for Employment Research, pp. 321–346.

Clark, Susan
1981   "Report on Indiana plant closings and job loss." Unpublished paper, Indianapolis: Citizens Action Coalition, August, 32 pp.

Cohn, Robert M.
1978   "The effect of employment status change on self-atti-
tudes." *Social Psychology,* 41:81–93.

Congressional Quarterly
1983   *Employment in America.* Washington D.C.: Congressional
Quarterly Inc.

Craypo, Charles
1984   "The deindustrialization of a factory town: Plant closings
and phasedowns in South Bend, Indiana, 1954–1983." *In*
Donald Kennedy (Ed.), *Labor and reindustrialization: Workers and corporate change.* University Park, PA: Pennsylvania
State University, pp. 27–67.

Craypo, Charles and Davisson, William I.
1983   "Plant shutdown, collective bargaining, and job and employment experiences of displaced brewery workers." *Labor Studies Journal,* 7:195–215.

Dahrendorf, Ralf
1959   *Class and class conflict in industrial society.* Stanford, CA:
Stanford University Press.
1964   "Recent changes in the class structure of European soci-
eties." *Daedalus,* 93:225–270.

DeFranzo, James
1973   "Embourgeoisement in Indianapolis?" *Social Problems,*
21:209–283.

Dollars and Sense
1982   "A long view of the economy in numbers." Vol. 78, pp.
10–11.

Dooley, David, Catalano, Ralph, Jackson, Robert, and Brownell, Ar-
lene
1981   "Economic, life, and symptom changes in a nonmetropol-
itan community." *Journal of Health and Social Behavior,*
22:144–154.

Dumas, Lloyd J.
1986   *The Overburdened Economy: Uncovering the causes of chronic*

unemployment, inflation, and national decline. Berkeley, CA: University of California Press.

Duncan, Otis, D., Schuman, Howard, and Duncan, Beverly
  1973   *Social change in a metropolitan community.* NY: Russell Sage foundation

Economic Notes
  1980a   "Focus on election platforms." Vol. 48 [9] (September): pp. 3–9.
  1980b   "Shutdowns," Vol. 48 [5] (May), pp. 3–9.
  1986   "Bargaining trends." Vol. 54, April–May, p. 1.

Ferman, Louis A.
  1984   "The political economy of human services: The Michigan case." *International Journal of Mental Health* 13:125–138.

Fisher, Jeff
  1982   "RCA workers 'applaud' termination agreement." *Monticello Herald Journal,* October 4, p. 1.

Fitzgerald, Pat
  1982   "Fountainhead of U.S.'s wealth poised for irreversible decline." *Crisis at the crossroads: Midwest economy.* Washington, D.C.: Gannet News Service, December, pp. 3–5.

Flaim, Paul O. and Sehgal, Ellen
  1985   "Displaced workers in 1979–83: How well have they fared?" *Monthly Labor Review, 108:*3–16.

Forbes
  1982   "Annual Directory Issue." Vol. 129 [10] (May 10), p. 286.
  1983   "Annual Directory." Vol. 131 [10] (May 9), p. 296.
  1984   "Annual Directory." Vol. 133 [10] (April 30), p. 236.

Fortune
  1982   "Splitting Up RCA." Vol. 105 (March 22), pp. 62–63.

Frank, Robert H. and Freeman, Richard T.
  1978   "The distributional consequences of direct foreign investment." *In* William G. Dewald (Ed.), *The impact of international trade and investment on employment, a conference of the U.S. Department of Labor,* Washington, D.C.: U.S. Government Printing Office, p. 156.

Friedman, Thomas L.
  1982   "RCA net off 26.9% in quarter." *New York Times,* January 28, Section IV, p. 1.

Fuchs, Riev
  1971   "Different meanings of unemployment for women." *Human Relations, 24:*495–499.

Gerard, Gary
  1982   "RCA hopes fade." *Logansport Pharos Tribune.* September
          30, p. 1.
Goldthorpe, John H., Lockwood, David, Bechhofer, Frank, and Platt,
Jennifer
  1968   *The affluent worker: Political attitudes and behavior.* Cam-
          bridge: Cambridge University Press.
Goodman, Robert
  1979   *The last entrepreneurs: America's regional wars for jobs and dol-
          lars.* Boston, MA: South End.
Gordus, Jeanne P.
  1984   "The human resource implications of plant shutdowns."
          American Academy of Political and Social Science, 475:66–79.
Gordus, Jeanne P., Jarley, Paul, and Ferman, Louis A.
  1981   *Plant closings and economic dislocation.* Kalamazoo, MI: W.
          E. Upjohn Institute for Employment Research.
Gore, Susan
  1978   "The effect of social support in moderating the health and
          consequences of unemployment." *Journal of Health and So-
          cial Behavior,* 19:157–65.
Haas, Gilda
  1985   *Plant-closures: Myths, realities and responses.* Boston, MA:
          South End Press.
Hainer, Marg and Koslofsky, Joanne
  1979   "Car wars." *NACLA Report on the Americas,* XIII:3–37.
Harris, Candee S.
  1984   "The Magnitude of job loss from plant closings and the
          generation of replacement jobs: Some recent evidence."
          The ANNALS, 475:15–28.
Hawley, James
  1978   "International banking and the internationalization of
          capital." *U.S. Capitalism in crisis.* New York: Union for
          Radical Political Economics, pp. 124–137.
Horowitz, David
  1971   *The free world colossus.* NY: Hill and Wang.
House, James S.
  1979   "Discussion." *In* Louis A. Ferman and Jeanne P. Gordus
          (Eds.), *Mental health and the economy.* Kalamazoo, MI: W.
          E. Upjohn Institute for Employment Research, pp. 315–
          320.
Indiana Employment Security Division
  1974–85   *Labor force estimate.* Indianapolis, IN.

1981   *Selected employment sectors.* Indianapolis, IN.
1985   *Indiana labor market trends.* Indianapolis, IN.
1980–84   *Indiana's Public Welfare Programs for Fiscal years, 1980, 1981, 1982, 1983, 1984.* Indianapolis, IN: Department of Public Welfare.

INDIRS
1984   The Indiana Information Retrieval System. Bloomington, IN: Indiana University.

Jackman, Mary R. and Jackman, Robert W.
1983   *Class awareness in the United States.* Berkeley, CA: University of California Press.

Jaffee, David
1986   "The political economy of job loss in the United States, 1970–1980." *Social Problems,* 33:297–315.

Kasl, Stanislav V. and Cobb, Sidney
1979   "Some mental health consequences of plant closings and job loss." *In* Louis A. Ferman and Jeanne P. Gordus (Eds.), *Mental health and the economy.* Kalamazoo, MI: W.E. Upjohn Institute for Employment Research, pp. 255–299.

Kasl, Stanislav V., Gore, Susan, and Cobb, Sidney
1975   "The experience of losing a job: Reported changes in health, symptoms and illness behavior." *Psychosomatic Medicine,* 37:106–22.

Kinichi, Angelo J.
1985   "Personal consequences of plant closings: A model and preliminary test." *Human Relations,* 38:197–212.

Kolko, Gabriel
1968   *The politics of war.* NY: Vintage.

Kolko, Joyce and Kolko, Gabriel
1972   *The limits of power.* NY: Harper and Row.

Krasner, Stephen D.
1982   "American policy and global economic stability." *In* William P. Avery and David P. Rapkin (Eds.), *America in a changing world political economy.* NY: Longman.

Larson, Jeffrey H.
1984   "The effects of husband's unemployment on marital and family relations in blue-collar families." *Family Relations,* 33:503–511.

Leggett, J. C.
1964   "Economic insecurity and working-class consciousness." *American Sociological Review,* 29:226–34.

Liem, G. Ramsey and Liem, Joan Huser

1979   "Social support and stress: Some general issues and their application to the problem of unemployment." *In* Louis A. Ferman and Jeanne P. Gordus (Eds.), *Mental health and the economy*. Kalamazoo, MI: W. E. Upjohn Institute for Employment Research, pp. 347–377.

Liem, Ramsey and Rayman, Paula
1982   "Health and social costs of unemployment: Research and policy considerations." *American Psychologist*, 37:1116–23.

Lipset, Seymour L. and Schneider, William
1983   *The confidence gap*. NY: Free Press.

Lipsky, Bruce
1979   *The labor market experience of workers displaced and relocated by plant shutdowns: The General Foods case*. NY: Garland.

Lynd, Staughton
1982   *The fight against shutdown: Youngstown's steel mill closings*. San Pedro, CA: Singlejack Books.

McDonough, Jeff
1982a   "RCA plant operation." *Monticello Herald Journal*. June 7, p. 1.
1982b   "Local RCA plant doomed." *Monticello Herald Journal*. July 23, p. 1.
1982c   "RCA factory workers given second chance." *Monticello Herald Journal*. August 20, p. 1.
1982d   "No indications RCA will stay." *Monticello Herald Journal*. September 3, 1982, p. 1.
1982e   "RCA ends ties with Monticello." *Monticello Herald Journal*. December 1, p. 1.

McKenzie, Richard B.
1984   *Fugitive industry: The economics and politics of deindustrialization*. San Francisco, CA: Pacific Institute for Public Policy Research.

Magdoff, Harry, and Sweezy, Paul M.
1981   "The deepening crisis of U.S. capitalism." *Monthly Review*, 33:1–17.

Mann, Michael
1973   *Consciousness and action among the western working class*. London: Macmillan.

Marshall, James R. and Funch, Donna P.
1979   "Mental illness and the economy: A critique and partial replication." *Journal of Health and Social Behavior*, 20:282–289.

Margolis, Louis H. and Farran, Dale C.

1984   "Unemployment and children." *International Journal of Mental Health* 13:107–124.

Mick, Stephen S.
1975   "Social and personal costs of plant shutdowns." *Industrial Relations* 14:203–208.

Mills, C. Wright
1959   *The sociological imagination.* NY: Oxford University Press.

Modelski, George. (Ed.)
1978   *Transnational corporations and world order.* San Francisco, CA: Freeman.

Monthly Labor Review
1984   "Current labor statistics." Vol. 107, p. 73.

Monticello Chamber of Commerce
1982   *Monticello, Indiana.*

Monticello Herald Journal.
1982   "RCA to idle 200 here." March 1, p. 1.

Morris, Robert T. and Murphy, Raymond J.
1966   "A paradigm for the study of class consciousness." *Sociology and Social Research,* 50:298–313.

Moskowitz, Milton, Katz, Michael, and Levering, Robert
1980   "RCA". *Everybody's business: An almanac.* NY: Harper and Row, pp. 844–848.

NACLA's Latin American and Empire Report
1975   *Hit and run: U.S. runaway shops on the Mexican border,* Vol. IX, pp. 1–31.

1977a   *Capital's flight: The apparel industry moves south.* Vol. XI, pp. 1–40.

1977b   *Electronics: The global industry,* Vol. XI, pp. 1–31.

New York Times
1986   "Low-paying jobs found rising." December 18, p. 18.

Nowak, Thomas C. and Snyder, Kay A.
1983   "Women's struggle to survive a plant shutdown." *The Journal of Intergroup Relations,* XI:24–44.

Office of Technology Assessment
1986   *Technology and structural unemployment: Reemploying displaced adults:* Washington, D.C.: Congress of the United States.

Organski, A.F.K.
1965   *World politics.* NY: Knopf.

Palen, J. John
1969   "Belief in government control and the displaced worker." *Administrative Science Quarterly,* 14:584–593.

Parkin, F.
  1971   Class inequality and political order. NY: Praeger.
Paterson, Thomas G.
  1973   *Soviet-American confrontation: Post-War reconstruction and the origins of the cold war.* Baltimore, MD: Johns Hopkins University.
Pearlin, Leonard I.
  1987   Personal communication. April 2.
Pearlin, Leonard I. and Schooler, Carmi
  1978   "The structure of coping." *Journal of Health and Social Behavior, 19*:2–21.
Pearlin, Leonard I., Lieberman, Morton A., Menaghan, Elizabeth G., and Mullan, Joseph T.
  1981   "The stress process." *Journal of Health and Social Behavior, 22*:337–56.
Perrucci, Carolyn C. and Targ, Dena B.
  1988   "Effects of a plant closing on marriage and family life." *In* Patricia Voydanoff and Linda Maika (Eds.), *Economic distress and families.* Beverly Hills, CA: Sage, in press.
Perrucci, Carolyn C. and Perrucci, Robert
  1986   "Unemployment and mental health: Research and policy implications." Paper presented at annual meetings of the Society for the Study of Social Problems.
Perrucci, Carolyn C., Perrucci, Robert, Targ, Dena B., and Targ, Harry R.
  1985   "Impact of a plant closing on workers and the community." *In* R. L. Simpson and I. H. Simpson (Eds.), *Research on the sociology of work: A research annual, Vol. III.* Greenwich, CT: JAI Press, pp. 231–260.
Perrucci, Carolyn C., Targ, Dena B., Perrucci, Robert, and Targ, Harry R.
  1987   "Plant closing: A comparison of the effects on female and male workers." *In* R. M. Lee (Ed.), *Redundancy, layoffs and plant closures: The social impact.* Beckenham, Kent, U.K.: Croom Helm Ltd. Publishers, pp. 181–207.
Pursell, Carroll W. (Ed.)
  1972   "Economic Concentration and World War II." *The military industrial complex.* NY: Harper and Row, pp. 151–171.
RCA
  1982   *Quarterly Review for Shareholders:* NY: Fourth Quarter.
  1983   *Annual Report,* New York, p. 31.
  1984   *Annual Report,* New York, pp. 39, 46.

RCA News
   1982   "RCA to close Monticello plant." RCA: Consumer Elec-
           tronics, Indianapolis, IN.
Rayman, Paula
   1982   "The world of not working: An evaluation of urban social
           service response to unemployment." *Journal of Health and
           Human Resources Administration*, 4:319–33.
Rinehart, James W.
   1971   "Affluence and the embourgeoisement of the working class:
           A critical look." *Social Problems, 19*:149–162.
Rosen, Ellen I.
   1983   "Laid off: Displaced blue collar women in New England."
           Paper presented at the annual meeting of the Society for
           the Study of Social Problems, Detroit, MI.
Rosenblum, Susan B.
   1984   "Healthcare and the unemployed." *Labor Research Review,
           5*:28–44.
Rothstein, Lawrence E.
   1986   *Plant closing: Power, politics and workers.* Dover, MA: Au-
           burn House.
Russell, Raymond
   1983   "Class formation in the workplace: The role of sources of
           income." *Work and Occupations, 10*:349–372.
Rytina, Joan H., Form, William H., and Pease, John
   1970   "Income and stratification ideology: beliefs about the
           American opportunity structure." *American Journal of So-
           ciology, 75*:703–16.
Sales and Marketing Management
   1981   "1981 Survey of Buying Power," Vol. 127 (July 27), pp.
           C-80, C-81.
   1982   "1982 Survey of Buying Power," Vol. 129 (July 26), pp.
           C-74, C-75.
   1983   "1983 Survey of Buying Power," Vol. 131 (July 25), pp.
           C-76.
   1984   "1984 Survey of Buying Power," Vol. 133 (July 23), pp.
           C-72, C-74.
Schlozman, Kay Lehman
   1979   "Women and unemployment: Assessing the biggest
           myths." *In* Jo Freeman (Ed.), *Women: A feminist perspective.*
           Palo Alto, CA: Mayfield, pp. 290–312.
Schlozman, Kay Lehman and Verba, Sidney
   1979   *Injury to insult: Unemployment, class, and political response.*
           Cambridge, MA: Harvard University Press.

Schulman, Michael D., Zingraff, Rhonda, and Reif, Linda
   1985   "Race, gender, class consciousness and union support: An analysis of southern textile workers." *Sociological Quarterly*, 26:187–204.
Schwefel, Detlef, Jurgen, John, Potthoff, Peter, and Hechler, Annerose
   1984   "Unemployment and mental health: Perspectives from the Federal Republic of Germany." *International Journal of Mental Health*, 13:35–50.
Seidman, Joel
   1953   *American labor from defense to reconversion.* Chicago, IL: University of Chicago.
Sennett, Richard and Cobb, Jonathan
   1972   *The hidden injuries of class.* NY: Random House.
Serrin, William
   1986   "Part-time work new labor trend," *New York Times*, July 9, pp. 1,9.
Shamir, Boas
   1985   "Sex differences in psychological adjustment to unemployment and reemployment: A question of commitment, alternatives or finance?" *Social Problems*, 33:67–79.
Silk, Leonard
   1982   "The Great Recession," *New York Times*, March 14, Section 3, p. 1.
Simpson, Ida H. and Simpson, Richard L. (Eds.)
   1982   *Research in the sociology of work: A research annual. Vol. 1: Worker consciousness.* Greenwich, CT: JAI Press.
Smith, David
   1984   "Industry stability counts: Economist." *Lafayette Journal and Courier.* January 8, p. 39.
Snyder, Kay A. and Nowak, Thomas C.
   1984   "Job loss and demoralization: Do women fare better than men?" *International Journal of Mental Health*, 13:92–106.
South Suburban Task Force on the Health Impact of Unemployment and Low Income
   1984   *The health impact of unemployment and low income.* Oak Park, IL: South Suburban Cook County - DuPage Health Systems Agency.
Spanier, John
   1980   *American foreign policy since World War II.* NY: Holt, Rinehart and Winston.
Stamas, George D.
   1984   "State and regional employment and unemployment in 1983." *Monthly Labor Review*, 107:9–15.

Tanner, Julian and Cockerill, Rhonda
   1986   "In search of working-class ideology: A test of two per-
             spectives." *Sociological Quarterly*, 27:389–402.
Targ, Dena B.
   1983   "Women and the new unemployment." *Humboldt Journal
             of Social Relations*, 10:47–60.
Targ, Harry R.
   1986   *Strategy of an empire in decline: Cold War II.* Minneapolis,
             MN: MEP.
United Nations
   1976–1980   *Statistical yearbook.* NY: Statistical Office of the United
                 Nations.
U.S. Department of Commerce Bureau of the Census
   1951, 1979, 1980, 1981   *Statistical Abstract of the United States,*
                               Washington, D.C.
Vanneman, Reeve and Pampel, Fred C.
   1977   "The American perception of class and status." *American
             Sociological Review*, 42:422–437.
Warr, Peter B.
   1978   "A study of psychological well-being." *British Journal of
             Psychology*, 69:111–121.
Warren, Rachelle (written by Anne E. Fisher)
   1978   "Unemployment, stress, and helping networks." *Women's
             worlds: NIMH supported research on women.* Washington,
             D.C.: U.S. Government Printing Office, pp. 96–99.
Weeks, Edward C. and Drengacz, Sandra
   1982   "The non-economic impact of community economic shock."
             Journal of Health and Human Resources Administration, 4:303–
             18.
Wilensky, Harold L. and Edwards, Hugh
   1959   "The skidder: Ideological adjustments of downward mo-
             bile workers." *American Sociological Review*, 24:215–231.
Williams, Winston
   1982   "Why business won't invest," *New York Times*, January
             31, Section 3, p. 1.
Zingraff, Rhonda and Schulman, Michael D.
   1984   "Social bases of class consciousness: A study of textile
             workers with a comparison by race." *Social Forces*, 63:98–
             116.

Midwest Plant Closing Project

CONFIDENTIAL

This questionnaire is concerned with the experiences of workers displaced by the closing of the RCA plant. The information that you give us can be used by organized labor and community agencies to help displaced workers around the country.

There are several points you should bear in mind while you are filling out the questionnaire.

1. *Your answers will be kept confidential.* Do not sign your name. A number appears at the top of this page. This number is used only to check the questionnaire returns. Once the questionnaire has been returned and we have no need to contact you again, this page will be torn off and discarded.
2. Read every question or statement carefully before answering. Please answer every question in accordance with the instructions. (Questions appear on both sides of each page.)
3. When you have completed the questionnaire, please return it in the enclosed self-addressed stamped envelope.

PLEASE COMPLETE AND RETURN AS SOON AS POSSIBLE.
THE RESULTS OF THIS STUDY WILL BE MADE AVAILABLE TO
YOU THROUGH YOUR UNION.

WE THANK YOU FOR YOUR COOPERATION IN THIS STUDY.

BACKGROUND INFORMATION
****

(01)   1. Where were you born?

_____1. Outside of Indiana

_____2. Indiana*

*What county:____1. White   1

                 ____2. Jasper

                 ____3. Carroll

                 ____4. Cass

                 ____5. Tippecanoe

                 ____6. Benton

                 ____7. Pulaski

                 ____8. Other county   1

2. What year were you born?   15-1

_____
    (year)

3. What is your sex? (check one)   1

_____1. Male

_____2. Female

4. What is the highest grade you completed in school? (please circle)
                                                                         18-1

    1 2 3 4 5 6 7 8   9 10 11 12   13 14 15 16
    _____ _____ _____
         Grade School   High School   College

5. What is your current marital status? (check one)   2

_____1. Single

_____2. Widowed

_____3. Divorced, separated

_____4. Married

HOUSEHOLD AND FAMILY
****

6. How many people live in your household? (write in number)   21-22

_____
(Number in household)

7. Please list the relationship of each person to you (for example, husband, son, mother, brother), and their age, sex, and employment status.

Relation to you	Age (years)	Sex (Circle one)		Presently employed (Circle one)		Did they work at RCA when plant closed?		
		(1)	(2)	(1)	(2)	(1)	(2)	
_____	_____	M	F	Yes	No	Yes	No	23-28
_____	_____	M	F	Yes	No	Yes	No	29-34
_____	_____	M	F	Yes	No	Yes	No	35-40
_____	_____	M	F	Yes	No	Yes	No	41-46
_____	_____	M	F	Yes	No	Yes	No	47-52
_____	_____	M	F	Yes	No	Yes	No	53-58
_____	_____	M	F	Yes	No	Yes	No	59-64

8. How many of your relatives live with 50 miles of your house? Include parents, children, in-laws, brothers and sisters, etc.

_____
(Number of relatives)   65-66

9. How many of your relatives lost their jobs at RCA because the plant closed?

_____
(Number of relatives)   67-68

EMPLOYMENT HISTORY
****

10. What was your job title at RCA at the time you were last laid off?

_____
(Write in your job title)   69-70

11. What was your annual income and your total family income (before
    taxes and deductions) in 1982?

    $_____
    (Your income in 1982)   71-7:

    $_____
    (Family income in 1982, you and your spouse)   73-7.

12. About how many times in the past ten years have you been unemployed
    or laid off for a month or more?

    _____1. Never   7:

    _____2. Once

    _____3. 2-3 times

    _____4. More than 3 times

13. Have you had any jobs since you were last laid off at RCA?

    _____1. No   7.

    _____2. Yes*

         *How many?_____   7'

14. Are you working now?

    _____1. No   7.

    _____2. Yes, full-time

    _____3. Yes, part-time

         What is your job title?_____   79-8.

(02) 15. How long have you had this job?

    _____
    (months)   05-0.

16. How much do you get paid?

    _____
    ($ per hour)   07-0!

    16A. How may hours do you work per week?

    _____
    (Hours worked per week, on average)   10-1:

YOUR OPINIONS
****

17. Here is a list of statements about the government. Check whether
    you agree or disagree with each statement.

	Agree (1)	Disagree (2)	
The government should end unemployment by hiring everybody who is without a job.	_____	_____	12
The government should see that every family has enough money to have a decent standard of living.	_____	_____	13
The government should reduce taxes on big business.	_____	_____	14
The government should tax the rich heavily in order to redistribute the wealth.	_____	_____	15
The government should limit the amount of money any individual is allowed to earn in a year.	_____	_____	16
The size of the government should be reduced even if it means cutting back on government services in areas such as health and education.	_____	_____	17

18. Do you think that the interests of management and workers are
    basically opposed or are their interests basically the same?

    ____1. Basically opposed   18

    ____2. Basically the same

    ____3. Mixed; depends; some interests conflict, others don't

    ____4. Don't know

19. Do you think that the child of a factory worker has about the same
    chance to get ahead as the child of a business executive, has somewhat
    less chance to get ahead, or much less chance to get ahead than the
    child of a business executive?

    ____1. About the same chance   19

    ____2. Somewhat less chance

    ____3. Much less chance

    ____4. Don't know

19A. Do you think that's fair?

    ____1. Yes   20

    ____2. No

    ____3. Don't know

20. What do you think are the two main reasons for the high unemployment
in the U.S.? Put a "1" by the most important cause and a "2" for
the second most important.

    ____ Big business   21

    ____ Unions   22

    ____ Government   23

    ____ Politicians   24

    ____ Welfare costs   25

    ____ Foreign competition   26

21. Here is a list of institutions in our society. For each one,
circle the number to show whether you now have a lot of confidence
in it, some confidence, or hardly any confidence at all.

	Lot of Confidence	Some Confidence	Hardly any Confidence	
Labor unions	1	2	3	27
Big business	1	2	3	28
Congress	1	2	3	29
The Supreme Court	1	2	3	30
The Presidency	1	2	3	31
The medical profession	1	2	3	32
The legal profession	1	2	3	33
Religious institutions	1	2	3	34
TV news shows	1	2	3	35
The schools	1	2	3	36
State legislature	1	2	3	37
Governor	1	2	3	38

22. Which one of the following groups do you think has the most
    influence on our government in Washington, D.C.?
    Which group do you think should have the most influence?
    In each column, put a "1" by the group that is most influential,
    and a "2" by the group this is second most influential.

Who has most influence?		Who should have most influence?
39) military leaders	(46)	military leaders
40) labor unions	(47)	labor unions
41) rich people	(48)	rich people
42) small businessmen	(49)	small businessmen
43) big business corporations	(50)	big business corporations
44) poor people	(51)	poor people
45) all groups are equal	(52)	all groups are equal

23. Do you agree or disagree with the following statements about why RCA
    closed the Monticello plant? (circle a number for each statement)

A. The RCA plant was not making a profit because of foreign competition.
   Management had little choice but to close down.

Strongly agree	Agree	Disagree	Strongly disagree	Don't know	
1	2	3	4	5	53

B. RCA was interested in increasing its profits. The Monticello
   plant was probably making money, but not as much as it could if
   it moved to a lower wage area.

Strongly agree	Agree	Disagree	Strongly disagree	Don't know	
1	2	3	4	5	54

C. RCA was under pressure to increase profits. They probably would
   have kept the plant open if the union would have agreed to large
   cuts in wages and benefits.

Strongly agree	Agree	Disagree	Strongly disagree	Don't know	
1	2	3	4	5	55

D. RCA is doing what many large corporation are doing. They are using the excuse of the recession to break the back of organized labor and get lower wages.

Strongly agree	Agree	Disagree	Strongly disagree	Don't know	
1	2	3	4	5	56

24. Listed below are some of the people and groups in your area that might have been helpful to unemployed workers after RCA closed. For each one, please check the space that best describes how concerned they were about the problems of unemployed RCA workers and how much help they gave.

	Very concerned & very helpful (1)	Concerned, but not very helpful (2)	Not concerned & not helpful (3)	
Mayor of Monticello	____	____	____	57
City Council of Monticello	____	____	____	58
Churches	____	____	____	59
Chamber of Commerce	____	____	____	60
Workers Aid Counsel (UBCJ #3154)	____	____	____	61
Monticello newspaper	____	____	____	62
U.S. Senators from Indiana	____	____	____	63
U.S. Representative from your district	____	____	____	64
Indiana State Senator	____	____	____	65
Indiana State Representative	____	____	____	66
State AFL-CIO	____	____	____	67
Social Service Agencies (Welfare Office; Township Trustees)	____	____	____	68
International Brotherhood of Carpenters and Joiners	____	____	____	69
Monticello banks	____	____	____	70

25. Here is a list of institutions in our society. For each one, indicate whether, since the plant closing, you have more confidence in it, less confidence, or the same.

	More confidence (1)	Less confidence (2)	Same as before (3)	
Labor unions	___	___	___	71
Big business	___	___	___	72
Congress	___	___	___	73
The Supreme Court	___	___	___	74
The Presidency	___	___	___	75
The medical profession	___	___	___	76
The legal profession	___	___	___	77
Religious institutions	___	___	___	78
TV news shows	___	___	___	79
The Schools	___	___	___	80
#3) State legislature	___	___	___	05
Governor	___	___	___	06

26. Listed below are some statements about the economy and your chances for a job in the future. Please check whether you agree or disagree with each statement.

	Agree (1)	Disagree (2)	Don't know (3)	
There is a good job waiting for me if I just look harder to find it.	___	___	___	07
No matter what I do it will be near impossible to find a job in the months ahead.	___	___	___	08
Finding a job is a matter of luck.	___	___	___	09
When the economy picks up, I will find a job easily.	___	___	___	10
I will soon be able to get a job even if the economy doesn't pick up.	___	___	___	11

UNION ACTIVITIES
****

27. During the last year you worked at RCA, how often did you attend
    the monthly meetings of Local #3154?

    ____1. At least once a month   12

    ____2. Almost every month

    ____3. About every other month

    ____4. A couple of times a year

    ____5. Hardly ever attended

28. Have you ever held any of the following union positions or been on a
    committee of Local #3154? (check all that apply)

    ____President   (13)   ____Treasurer   (17)

    ____Committee chairperson (14)   ____Secretary   (18)

    ____Committee member   (15)   ____Other   (19)

    ____Steward   (16)
                                        _____
                                                       (write in)

29. Since the RCA plant closed, have you ever called upon the Workers
    Aid Counsel for help, advice, or information?

    ____1. No   20

    ____2. Yes*

        * If Yes, about how many times? _____   21-22
                                        (write in number of times)

30. How did you feel about the union at RCA before there was any talk of
    closing the plant? How much did they help the workers on things like
    wages, health benefits, retirement benefits, and grievances?
    (check one for each wage-benefit)

	A big help to workers (1)	Helped some but not enough (2)	Not much help (3)	
Wages	_____	_____	_____	23
Health benefits	_____	_____	_____	24
Retirement benefits	_____	_____	_____	25
Grievances	_____	_____	_____	26

31. How satisfied are you with the terms of the closing contract your
     union negotiated with RCA? (circle a number for <u>each</u> item)

	Very satisfied	Satisfied	Dissatisfied	Very dissatisfied	
ealth insurance	1	2	3	4	27
ife insurance	1	2	3	4	28
everance pay	1	2	3	4	29
etirement option	1	2	3	4	30

FAMILY LIFE AND HEALTH
****

32. Unemployment usually results in financial pressure. This can produce
     problems in relationships with spouse, children, family, and friends.
     How did the financial pressure of unemployment affect your relation-
     ships? (check one in <u>each</u> column)

Relationships with spouse (31)	Relationships with children (32)	Relationships with family (33)	Relationships with friends (34)
____1.Not married	____1.No children	____1.No family	____1.No friends
____2.Better	____2.Better	____2.Better	____2.Better
____3 No change	____3.No change	____3.No change	____3.No change
____4 Worse	____4.Worse	____4.Worse	____4.Worse

33. In order to make ends meet since you were laid off, are you
     spending more time on any of the following activities? (check <u>all</u>
     that apply)

_____ Shopping for food bargains   35

_____ Shopping for clothing bargains   36

_____ Preparing meals   37

_____ Gardening   38

_____ Canning   39

_____ Making and mending clothes   40

_____ Home repairs   41

_____ Auto repairs   42

_____ Taking care of children   43

34. Please check any of the following that happened to you <u>due</u> to your layoff from RCA.

____ Headaches (44)   ____ Loss of appetite (50)

____ Stomach trouble (45)   ____ Drinking more (51)

____ Heart trouble (46)   ____ Smoking more (52)

____ Trouble breathing (47)   ____ Lack of energy (53)

____ High blood pressure (48)   ____ Other (54)

____ Trouble sleeping (49)   _____
                                                    (specify)

35. During the <u>past week</u>, how often did you:

	Very often (1)	Somewhat often (2)	Not often or never (3)	
Lack enthusiasm for doing anything?	____	____	____	55
Have an appetite?	____	____	____	56
Feel lonely?				57
Feel bored or have little interest in doing things?	____	____	____	58
Lose sexual interest or pleasure?	____	____	____	59
Have trouble getting to sleep or staying asleep?	____	____	____	60
Cry easily or feel like crying?	____	____	____	61
Feel downhearted or blue?	____	____	____	62
Feel like throwing things?	____	____	____	63
Feel low in energy or slowed down?	____	____	____	64
Feel hopeless about the future?	____	____	____	65
Feel like screaming or shouting?	____	____	____	66
Feel like hitting someone or something?	____	____	____	67

36. How strongly do you agree or disagree with <u>each</u> of these statements about yourself?

	Strongly agree (1)	Agree (2)	Disagree (3)	Strongly disagree (4)	
There is really no way I can solve some of the problems I have	____	____	____	____	68
Sometimes I feel that I'm being pushed around in life	____	____	____	____	69
I have little control over the things that happen to me	____	____	____	____	70
I can do just about anything I really set my mind to	____	____	____	____	71
I often feel helpless in dealing with the problems of life	____	____	____	____	72
What happens to me in the future depends mostly on me	____	____	____	____	73
There is little I can do to change many of of the important things in my life	____	____	____	____	74

37. Listed below are three different kinds of relationships with family and friends. Check the one statement that describes you.

    ____ 1. I have a lot of love and support from family and friends.

    ____ 2. I have sympathetic friends and family but they don't always listen and give support.

    ____ 3. I don't have many people to provide me with support or sympathy.   75

38. You may have had to make some adjustments in your living expenses when you became unemployed at the RCA plant. Which, if any, of the following expenses were affected? (omit checking those that don't apply)

	Eliminated (1)	Reduced (2)	No change (3)	Increased (4)	
a. Health insurance	____	____	____	____	7(
b. Life insurance	____	____	____	____	7'
c. Fire insurance	____	____	____	____	7(
d. Auto insurance	____	____	____	____	7(
e. Dental care	____	____	____	____	8(

(04)

f. Health care	____	____	____	____	0(
g. Food	____	____	____	____	0(
h. Telephone	____	____	____	____	0(
i. Magazines or newspaper	____	____	____	____	0(
j. Clothing	____	____	____	____	0(
k. Home upkeep and repair	____	____	____	____	1(
l. Auto upkeep and repair	____	____	____	____	1(
m. Entertainment	____	____	____	____	1(
n. Charitable contributions	____	____	____	____	1(
o. Gifts	____	____	____	____	14
p. Children's schooling	____	____	____	____	1(
q. Children's other expenses	____	____	____	____	1(
r. Child support/alimony	____	____	____	____	1(
s. Your education/training	____	____	____	____	1(
t. Rent, house payments	____	____	____	____	1(

u. Other (specify)

_____ 2(

39. In which of the expenses listed in Question 38 above, if any, do you think the next cutbacks will be during the coming months? (specify letters of expense areas)

_____ 21-41

40. Do you have a paid-up house mortgage?

_____ 1. No, I rent   42

_____ 2. No, I'm still paying the mortgage

_____ 3. Yes, I do

41. Since the RCA plant closed, how have you been meeting or paying for your living expenses? Please check all the sources of income you have at present.

_____ Your own present job   43

_____ Spouse's salary   44

_____ Unemployment compensation (own)   45

_____ Unemployment compensation (spouse)   46

_____ Pensions (including Social Security)   47

_____ Food stamps   48

_____ Public assistance   49

_____ Child support or alimony   50

_____ Severance pay from RCA   51

_____ Savings   52

_____ Rental income   53

_____ Income from investments   54

_____ Borrowing on life insurance   55

_____ Borrowing from family or friends   56

_____ Borrowing on house mortgage   57

_____ Other income source (specify)

_____

_____   58

42. At the present time:

	Yes	No
Are you able to afford a home suitable for yourself/your family?	____	____
Are you able to afford furniture or household equipment that needs to be replaced?	____	____
Are you able to afford the kind of car you need?	____	____
Do you have enough money for the kind of food you/your family should have?	____	____
Do you have enough money for the kind of clothing you/your family should have?	____	____
Do you have enough money for the kind of leisure activities you/your family wants?	____	____
Do you have a great deal of difficulty paying your bills?	____	____
At the end of the month do you end up with money left over?	____	____

WE KNOW THAT HIS HAS BEEN A LONG QUESTIONNAIRE AND WE APPRECIATE THE TIME YOU SPENT COMPLETING IT. WE WOULD LIKE TO GIVE YOU A CHANCE TO ADD ANYTHING ELSE YOU WANT ON HOW YOU HAVE BEEN AFFECTED BY THE CLOSING AND WHETHER YOUR FEELINGS ABOUT YOUR UNION, YOUR COMMUNITY, OR YOUR GOVERNMENT HAVE CHANGED. (write below or on back of first page)

INDEX

189